MW01228650

Unfuck

Your

Anxiety

By Evette Rose

Edition 1

ISBN: 9798373815833

Disclaimer

All information obtained from Evette Rose, or anything written or said by her, is to be taken solely as advisory in nature. Evette Rose and Metaphysical Anatomy™ will not be held personally, legally, or financially liable for any action taken based upon their advice. Evette Rose is not a psychologist or medical professional and is unable to diagnose, prescribe, treat, or cure any ailment. Anyone using the information in this book acknowledges that they have read and understand the details of this disclaimer. Evette can discuss the metaphysical explanations for psychological disorders but are unable to diagnose, prescribe, treat, or claim to cure any illnesses that require medical or psychiatric attention. The principles taught in Metaphysical Anatomy™ and in this book is based on Evette's life experiences and are guidelines and suggestions to support those seeking simple tools to improve their quality of life. By utilizing and using this book, the participant acknowledges that he/she assumes full responsibility for the knowledge gained herein and its application. Material in this book is not intended to replace the advice of a competent healthcare practitioner. The reader takes full responsibility for the way they utilize and exercise the information in this book.

Legal

All recordings and publications obtained from Evette Rose, or this book remain the intellectual property of the aforementioned and must not be used or reprinted in any way without the written permission of Evette Rose. Any unauthorized commercial use of Evette Rose's name, photograph, images, or written material is strictly prohibited and is in direct violation of rights.

ACKNOWLEDGMENTS

Thank you to each and every client or student that I have met for your insight, support, and willingness to share your life stories. I would not have been able to write this book without you! Thank you, Noemi Idang, for your unconditional support!

With Love,
Evette Rose

Unfuck Your Anxiety

Also by the author

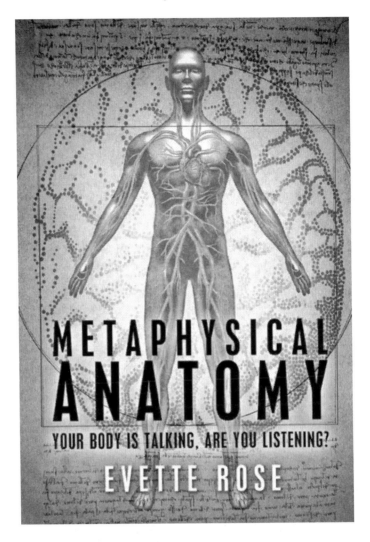

Metaphysical Anatomy is about 679 illnesses from A – Z. This book is so much more than the emotional components of each disease. Metaphysical Anatomy also includes step-by-step guide for identifying the origin of the disease process, whether it be in your ancestry, conception, womb, birth, or childhood. This book is equally valuable for experienced alternative healing practitioners, psychotherapists, hypnotherapists, personal development coaches and those interested in self-healing.

Psychosomatics Of Children
Your Ancestry is talking
Are you Listening?

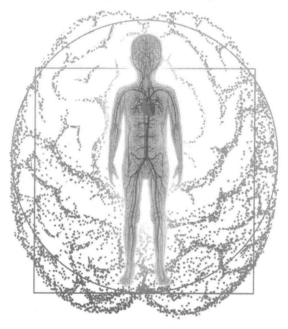

Evette Rose
METAPHYSICAL ANATOMY VOLUME 3

Psychosomatics of children is the sister book of metaphysical anatomy volume one. This book focuses on children's ailments and psychological challenges. Children have not had a full life yet. Therefore, ailments in their bodies are stemming from womb and ancestral trauma, which is unresolved. Not only is your body talking in this book, but your ancestry is talking, are you listening?

Unfuck your trauma, instincts, sabotage, habits, pain, addictions, patterns, values, consciousness, and awareness. It's time to get back to who you really are! This book is for people who want to change their lives but don't know where to start or what steps to take first, because they have never looked at themselves before, or because they have tried everything else and failed so badly that they feel like a failure and it's easier not to try again than risk failing again, which would make them feel even more of a failure. You are not destined for failure! You are destined for greatness!

Metaphysical Anatomy Technique Volume 2 explains the core foundation and healing technique behind Metaphysical Anatomy Volume 1 which describes step-by-step guide for identifying the psychosomatic pattern related to 679 medical conditions. These conditions can be activated by circumstances in your present life, your ancestry, conception, womb, birth trauma, childhood, or adult life. Volume 2 teaches you the foundation of Volume 1 including a powerful healing technique. There is also an Online Healing Course that you can combine with Volume 1 and Volume 2.

DEPRESSION DOESN'T HAVE TO BE A LIFE SENTENCE IF YOU ARE THE JUDGE.

UNFUCK
YOUR
DEPRESSION
Evette Rose

Depression can be a heavy, difficult-to-lift weight. It can sap your energy and make it hard to motivate yourself. But depression is a real condition that often requires treatment. There are many different types of depression, with various causes. Some people experience depression in response to a specific event, while others have ongoing, long-term problems that contribute to their depression. Depression can affect anyone, regardless of age, race, or gender. It's not always easy to recognize, but there are ways to get help. In this book, I share how I unfucked my depression.

A NEW SELF-HELP BOOK THAT CAN HELP

UN*UCK

YOUR

PAIN

Evette Rose

"Unfuck Your Pain is a book about pain and how to deal with it. Chronic pain affects millions of people worldwide, but there's still so much we don't understand about it. Our goal for this book is to give you the tools you need to understand with your own pain, as well as share some of our findings from research on the topic." If you're suffering from psychosomatic pain, emotional pain, or any other type of ailment pain, Unfuck your Pain can help you understand your pain from a new perspective. The Psychosomatics of pain refer to the idea that our thoughts and emotions can contribute to pain. For example, someone who is constantly worrying about their pain may find that their pain gets worse. Our understanding of pain has come a long way, especially in my research. In this book, I will share my research regarding pain, chronic pain, and psychosomatic pain.

MANIFESTING DOESN'T WORK, BUT THIS WILL!

UN**F**UCK

YOUR

FINANCES

Evette Rose

Unfuck your finances to create prosperity and abundance. Manifest success and heal blocks to abundance with this powerful financial tool. Get clear about your values and ancestry to empower your financial future. Create awareness around your relationship to money for lasting change. This is a great guide to getting your money in order and becoming successful. Get blocks off your energy and start achieving your goals with this helpful guide to financial awareness. Heal your relationship with money and achieve abundance with this valuable guide to financial ancestry. Discover your values and manifest wealth with this enlightening guide to financial success If you can resolve and release these issues, you will open yourself up to a more prosperous future. Once you identify your blocks, you can start working on resolving them. With a little effort, you can transform your finances and set yourself up for prosperity.

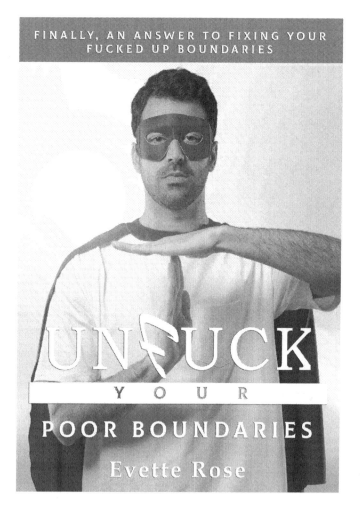

FINALLY, AN ANSWER TO FIXING YOUR
FUCKED UP BOUNDARIES

UN UCK
Y O U R
POOR BOUNDARIES
Evette Rose

"Unfuck your poor boundaries" is a self-help book that will help you reclaim your life. It's a guide to understanding and setting healthy boundaries and learning to say no when you need to. If you've ever felt trapped or held back by your relationships, this is the book for you. "Unfuck your poor boundaries" is funny, relatable, and packed with information that will change your life for the better. If you're tired of feeling like you're constantly walking on eggshells, it's time to get your boundaries back! This book will help you set healthy limits and finally start living the life you deserve. build resilience and thrive in the face of adversity, this is the book for you!

Unfuck Your Happiness is a life-changing book that will show you how to be happy. It's packed with powerful techniques and strategies that will help you overcome unhappiness and trauma. You'll finally be able to find your purpose in life and achieve your birthright to happiness. This book is funny, engaging, and easy to read - perfect for anyone who wants to start living a happier life today! It's a guide to overcoming trauma and negative associations that hold you back from happiness.

LEARN TO COMMUNICATE EFFECTIVELY AND GET WHAT YOU WANT

UN**F**UCK
Y O U R
COMMUNICATION
Evette Rose

Unfuck Your Communication is a communication tool designed to help you become more effective and successful at communicating with others. It is based on the premise that most people have some sort of block when it comes to communicating effectively. By becoming aware of these blocks, you can resolve them and improve the way you communicate with other people. This will lead to better relationships, more success in your career, and greater happiness overall.

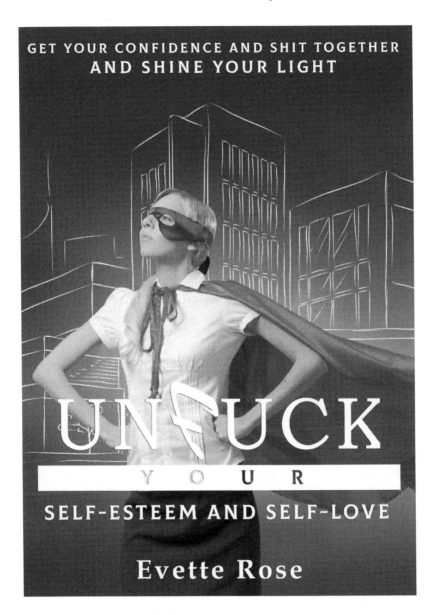

Unfuck Your Self-esteem and Self-love is a book that will help you release your past self-sabotaging patterns, clear out your negative associations with yourself, heal your confidence, and more. This book is all about finding love for yourself, no matter what you've been through. It's about learning to forgive yourself for the things that have happened to you in the past or even recently. It's about letting go of old stories that keep you stuck. It's time to shine your fucking light!

HOW TO MAKE YOUR BREAK-UP
SUCK A LITTLE BIT LESS

UNFUCK

YOUR

HEART

Evette Rose

Unfuck Your Heart is a funny and poignant guide for turning your life around after a relationship. It includes exercises that will help you discover the root of your problems and give you tools for moving forward with grace and ease. This book is for anyone who has ever questioned their self-worth or felt lost in love. Unfuck your heart is a self-help book that helps you heal from heartbreak, divorce, relationship challenges, and abuse. It shows you how to manifest the love of your life and values into your life. This book helps you change the negative patterns in your life, such as sabotage and regret.

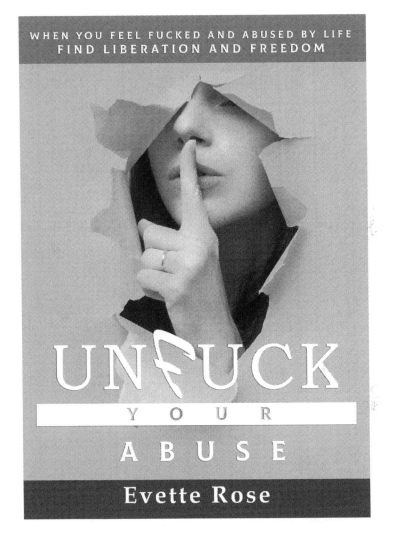

WHEN YOU FEEL FUCKED AND ABUSED BY LIFE
FIND LIBERATION AND FREEDOM

UNFUCK
YOUR
ABUSE
Evette Rose

Are you tired of being abused? It's time to break the silence! I can relate because that person used to be me. In this book share my life story, the good the bad and ugly. Being raised in a violent home along with a drug addicted, alcoholic parent trying to navigate my way through what seemed to be the beginning of the end. Unfuck Your Abuse is here to help you heal from the trauma of abuse and become the confident person you were meant to be. We offer a unique combination of trauma healing, self-sabotage patterns, and abuse pattern identification that will help you let go of the past and move forward with your life. If you're ready to take control of your life and heal the wounds of your past, click here to learn more about our program.

This true-life story is a must-read for people who have either experienced abuse or care about someone else who may be trapped in processing their childhood experiences. This book brings an empowering message of hope, healing and understanding to anyone who feels challenged by their past.

This is a powerful book with a sobering insight to life's bullshit. It provides you with tools and insights you need to work through life's conundrums. This book offers a variety of topics, such as anxiety, depression, self-esteem, communication, boundaries, anger, unhappiness, pain, abundance fuck-ups, relationship conundrums, childhood, parent issues and so much more! The goal of this book is to give you an empowering kick up your ass to find liberation, understanding, and healing. I, myself, have been through my shitshow and I will share powerful insights and research that helped me to turn my life around. This book is part of a 14-book series. You are just scratching the surface

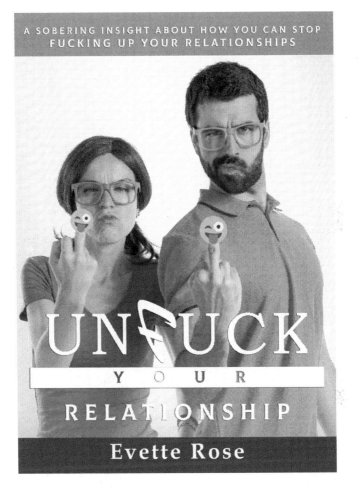

A SOBERING INSIGHT ABOUT HOW YOU CAN STOP
FUCKING UP YOUR RELATIONSHIPS

UN UCK
Y O U R
RELAT ONSHIP
Evette Rose

Unfuck Your Relationships is a hilarious guide to healing relationships, trauma, anger in relationships and gaslighting. If you're dealing with a narcissist or controlling partner, this book has the solutions you need. Figure out your shit and language for love, boundaries, dating, marriage, and more. Learn about the language of love and boundaries so that you can communicate effectively with anyone in your life. Unfuck Your Relationships provides tools to help you heal from narcissistic abuse by learning how to recognize gaslighting. This book will also help you understand abuse and control games in your relationships. It will teach you how to set boundaries, communicate effectively, and love yourself. You'll learn how to identify if your relationship has toxic elements in it and how to know when someone is gaslighting you or abusing you emotionally or verbally. Unfuck Your Relationships are also funny.

Evette Rose

Transform Everyday

Metaphysical Anatomy Quotes For Inspiration

The healing intention of this book is to create awareness of your blocks and patterns. It is through awareness that healing, and transformation takes place. In this book you will find quotes and inspirations designed to heal and transform every day of the year.

Table of Contents

Getting started

Hi, my name is Evette Rose and welcome to my world. I look forward to starting this journey with you to dive deep into challenges that you might be having in your life. Congratulations for taking active steps to improve your quality of life it takes courage to make a decision, but it takes determination to follow through on the decision that you made. Know that during this journey you are exactly where you need to be.

I invite you to move through this book with ease and with grace with an open mind and let go of taking life so seriously.

I would love to stay in touch with you and you can join me on any of my events I always have weekly free master classes and free mini workshops.

You can join me on social media hang out have fun and enjoy a tremendous amount of free content that I also share.

Find me at:

Free MAT Membership site: www.matmembers.com

Free Masterclasses: www.matmasterclass.com

IG: evetteroseofficial

IG: unfuckyourlifeofficial

Youtube: www.evettevideos.com

Events: www.evetterose.com

Unfuck Your Anxiety

Introduction

Anxiety is a feeling of worry, nervousness, or unease about something with an uncertain outcome. This feeling can be mild to severe. It's natural to feel anxious when we're facing a challenging situation, such as taking a test or giving a presentation. Anxiety can be referred to as a fear of the unknown. Anxiety causes a sense of insecurity and uncertainty.

It can also be referred to as a stress response to a perceived threat. It causes the brain to be caught up in feelings of stress and apprehension, which can cause anticipation, panic, and excessive worry. Everyone has experienced anxiety at some point in their life. It can be a normal stress reaction. For example, a person might feel anxious about difficult decision-making before taking a test or setting an exam, etc. but for people with an anxiety disorder, the anxiety does not go away and can get worse. It can interfere with work, school, and personal relationships.

Anxiety is the body's natural response to situations that are interpreted as threatening. Almost everyone knows what it is like to feel anxious. For example, if you are driving your car too fast on the highway, anxiety might give you a warning to slow down the car. Without anxiety, people would make a lot of poor decisions as they would stop interpreting anything as threatening. This can cause people to act irrationally. Anxiety can also help people cope with situations by giving them a boost of energy or helping them focus. Anxiety causes people to take action and face threatening situations.

It can even make people study harder for an exam. But for people with anxiety disorders, the feelings of uneasiness, dread, and fear are not temporary. They do not go away with time. This feeling of uneasiness and dread can be very overwhelming for people who suffer from anxiety disorders. The symptoms can interfere with their daily life activities, such as their performance at jobs, school, or relationships. Anxiety can help people cope, but for people who suffer from an anxiety disorder, this normally helpful emotion can be very harmful. This I can personally speak of experience. To be even frank, if I may, anxiety fucking ruined my life!

It's a mind-fuck of an experience, but we live through this shitshow every day. I applaud you for showing up every day. I know how hard it is to push through this, but here we are, you and me right now, giving anxiety the middle finger. You have made it through each day successfully!

Chapter 1

Experiencing anxiety

This disorder is a crippling experience to have. It can prevent a person from coping with normal, basic life routines. Their disorder makes them feel anxious all the time for no apparent reason. For some people, these feelings can be so overwhelming and uncomfortable that they can stop them from several daily life activities. People who suffer from anxiety disorder can have such severe bouts of anxiety that it can terrify them and immobilize them. Anxiety disorders are the most common type of mental health disorder.

It is also possible that anxiety is experienced at an exceptionally low level of intensity. This kind of intensity can cause a person to feel uneasy. I call this silent anxiety, and it's like walking on a goddamn minefield. A person will probably ignore this kind of anxiety, but eventually, the effects increase, and it will give you a kick up your ass.

A survey done in the United States proves that anxiety disorder is a very common type of mental health disorder. According to the survey, 5.3 million people suffer from anxiety per year. 5.2 million people suffer from post-traumatic stress disorder per year. Specific phobias affect over 1 out of every 10 people.

Obsessive-compulsive disorders affect every 2 to 3 people out of 100. Twice as many women suffer from anxiety disorders as men.

People suffering from anxiety can also feel that they are about to get sick or that they are about to experience harm. It can cause people to feel that they are experiencing fatal harm concerned to their emotional or physical well-being. It can also cause people to feel breathless and numb, or it can also cause their heartbeat to race. Some people also experience imagining dreadful situations. They play these situations in their heads with the worst potential outcomes. Anxiety can cause people to engage in internal dialogues, and they can play situations in their heads as if they were completely real.

People who experience anxiety often end up subconsciously and unintentionally creating situations they fear. It does not mean that what they fear always comes true, but they can create a self-fulfilling prophecy. This can be explained by the example of a person who fears that someone will abandon them, so they end the relationship themselves. Why? They hate the anticipation of waiting for the other shoe to drop and to be rejected. So, often they pull the trigger first. They can also act in ways that will cause them to be rejected.

It is a common phenomenon that if we keep telling a playing child that they will fall, eventually, they end up falling. This does not always happen because we are right in the first place, but by repeating to the child that they will fall, we make them believe that they will, so they stop being careful about it, and it creates a self-fulfilling prophecy.

Types of anxiety disorders

Anxiety can come forward in many shapes, forms, sensations, and reactions. There are different anxiety disorders. There are common types, such as anxiety disorder, panic disorder, separation anxiety, compulsions, and phobias.

Generalized anxiety disorder

People with GAD worry excessively about everyday things like health, money, family, work, or school. They are worried about these common things, and this worry is not trivial but excessive. They have had these thoughts almost every day for at least six months. It is common to worry about everyday life problems such as giving an exam or an interview. Some amount of stress also helps us if they are at a manageable level, but a person who is living with a generalized anxiety disorder experiences a lot of worry and anxiety for a long period. There is no apparent reason for the anxiety.

These feelings are uncontrollable, and people rarely know that they are suffering from that kind of anxiety. Even trivial things, such as completing daily tasks, can make people suffering from generalized anxiety disorder feel anxious. It is important to note that the amount of worry people suffering from generalized anxiety disorder feel is not normal, and differs from occasional worrying. Generalized anxiety disorder develops slowly. The most common age around which generalized anxiety disorder can develop is around 30. However, it can also develop during childhood.

This disorder is more common in women than in men. An intense fear of social situations, such as public speaking, characterizes social anxiety disorder or meeting new people. They characterize panic disorder as unexpected and repeated episodes of intense fear accompanied by physical symptoms like heart palpitations, sweating, shaking, shortness of breath, dizziness, or nausea.

The symptoms of generalized anxiety disorder are like any other anxiety disorder, but the most common symptoms are feeling irritable, getting startled easily, and having trouble concentrating. Worrying excessively about normal daily activities and physical symptoms such as fatigue, nausea, headaches, sweating, shortness of breath, dizziness, and body aches are also symptoms of GAD. People with a generalized anxiety disorder have trouble controlling their worries or feelings of nervousness. They are often aware of the fact that they worry more than they should, but they have no control over it.

They have trouble relaxing, and they feel restless all the time. People with generalized anxiety disorder also have a hard time falling and staying asleep. Does insomnia sound familiar? It can also affect their daily life activities, such as school and work. Generalized anxiety disorder causes people to worry about natural catastrophes like earthquakes or wars. They are excessively worried about the health of loved ones and family members. Symptoms of generalized anxiety disorder can fluctuate over time, and they can also worsen during times of stress in life.

The exact cause of generalized anxiety disorder is still unknown. It is usually a combination of psychological, social, and biological factors. Other factors which can cause generalized anxiety disorder have been linked to genetics. The risk of generalized anxiety disorder runs in families. It is possible that generalized anxiety disorder can be inherited. Daily stress and work pressure can also cause this kind of anxiety. Researchers have also found that external causes, such as experiencing a traumatic event or being constantly in a stressful environment, can also put an individual at high risk of developing a generalized anxiety disorder.

Social anxiety

An intense fear of social situations, such as public speaking, characterizes social anxiety disorder. Social anxiety is a kind of disorder in which a person experiences fear at social gatherings.

People with social anxiety also feel anxious when they are exposed to unfamiliar people or situations in which they have to interact with unfamiliar people. It is important to note that social anxiety differs from shyness, which can go away with time, but social anxiety does not. It also affects daily life activities. It is normal to worry about social situations, but people who suffer from social anxiety feel overly worried about them.

Symptoms of social anxiety disorders are mostly related to social interactions. For people who suffer from social anxiety disorders, social interactions can lead to blushing, nausea, sweating, trembling, shaking, rigid body stance, difficulty speaking, feeling as if their mind is going blank, dizziness, rapid heartbeat, lightheadedness, and other physical symptoms of anxiety. Some other symptoms of social anxiety can also be intense worry about facing social situations and trying to blend into the background.

The exact causes of social anxiety are unknown, but it can result from a combination of various physical, biological, and genetic factors. I have a few strong opinions because of my extensive research relating to this condition. However, considering science, some problems with neurotransmitter systems can lead to imbalances in hormones, such as serotonin and dopamine. These imbalances can cause various psychological problems because they help regulate mood. Social anxiety disorder can also develop because of emotional, physical, or other abuse. Problems during childhood, such as over-controlling parents or childhood trauma, can also lead to social anxiety. Social anxiety also runs in families, but it is not clear whether it is because of environmental factors or genetics.

Panic disorder

Panic disorder is characterized by unexpected and repeated episodes of intense fear accompanied by physical symptoms like heart palpitations, sweating, shaking, shortness of breath, dizziness, or nausea. There are periods of intense fear and discomfort in which a person experiences physical symptoms of anxiety. It can cause a person to feel detached from themselves or their body. People fear they are losing control or going crazy. People suffering from panic attacks can also feel as if they are dying. The physical symptoms are so intense that they can feel like a heart attack. Panic attacks can occur even when there is no evident threat present. They can come on quickly and can last several minutes or more.

Panic attacks are sudden! They usually start slowly and peak within 10 minutes, then they might disappear soon. Physical signs of a panic attack include chills, choking sensation, difficulty breathing, fear of losing control, nausea, high heart rate, sweating, tingling, trembling, shaking, and intense fear of terror. Later in this book, I will teach you kick-ass techniques that had a profound impact on my life.

Anxiety disorders such as panic disorders can run in the family. However, it is not confirmed by researchers if they are genetic or not. In my research, I am leaning strongly towards saying that it can be inherited! Depression and other mental illnesses can also make a person prone to panic attacks. Substance abuse, such as alcoholism and drug addiction, also increases the risk of panic attacks.

Agoraphobia

Agoraphobia is an intense fear of being in situations where escape might be difficult or embarrassing, such as being in a crowd or on a bridge. It is a feeling of anxiousness about being in a place or situation where the person might find it difficult to escape or where they cannot get any help. People who are suffering from agoraphobia avoid being in crowds, standing in lines, on bridges, or on physical transportation. Agoraphobia usually starts before the age of 35. It is more common among women. And roughly 2% of adults experience it in the United States.

The physical symptoms of agoraphobia include chest pain, rapid heart rate, feeling shaky, having an intense feeling of fear, dizziness, lightheadedness, hyperventilation, trouble breathing, flushing, excessive sweating, and upset stomach.

Panic attacks and other phobias increase the risk of agoraphobia. Stressful life events can also trigger agoraphobia.

Some people have nervous and anxious nature, and they are more prone to developing agoraphobia. Research has also found that having a relative with agoraphobia also makes a person more prone to developing it. Agoraphobia is associated with existing panic attacks.

Phobias

In phobias, people have an intense fear of something that poses little or no harm at all. This fear can be about heights, social gatherings, spiders, etc. These fears are irrational and excessive. People with phobias avoid the feared situations; they might endure it but with great distress. If exposed to such situations which they fear, they experience intense anxiety responses. According to an estimate, almost 19 million Americans have a phobia that affects their daily lives.

Different phobias have different symptoms. I have previously discussed agoraphobia, along with its symptoms. Social phobia is also referred to as social anxiety disorder, and the symptoms are very much alike. People who suffer from social phobia have difficulty facing social situations. People who suffer from claustrophobia are afraid of closed or enclosed spaces. People who suffer from height phobia or acrophobia are afraid of being at a place with high altitude.

Glossophobia is characterized as performance anxiety or the fear of speaking in front of an audience. People who suffer from aviophobia have a fear of flying. Dental phobia is a fear of dentists and dental procedures. Nyctophobia makes people afraid of nighttime and darkness. There are a lot of phobias, and the symptoms of all of them vary. But a common symptom of phobia is a panic attack. The physical symptoms are like that of panic attacks, such as shortness of breath, dry mouth, nausea, elevated blood pressure, chest pain, racing heart, dizziness, and a choking sensation.

Several genetic and environmental factors have been linked to causing phobias. Research has also found that people with a close relative who has a phobia are more likely to develop that kind of phobia. Distressing events such as traumatic experiences can also cause a person to develop a phobia. People with ongoing medical conditions are also prone to developing phobias. Substance abuse and depression are also connected to phobias.

Obsessive-compulsive disorder

Obsessive-Compulsion disorder is a pattern of unwanted thoughts and fears which leads you to do repetitive behaviors. These repetitive behaviors are known as compulsions. Compulsions are defined as repetitive behaviors, such as repetitive hand washing, repetitively checking something, or ordering something. These repetitive behaviors can also be mental acts, such as counting, repeating words silently, or praying. People with compulsions feel that they have to perform these repetitive behaviors to reduce anxiety and distress. This also includes preventing a situation or event they are afraid of.

Although the goal of compulsion is not to provide pleasure or gratification, instead, it is to prevent a dreaded event or situation. These obsessions are characterized by persistent thoughts, impulses, or ideas. It is characterized by the person feeling that they do not have any kind of control over the thoughts they are having. Obsessive-compulsive disorders center on certain themes, such as the fear of getting contaminated by germs, which leads you to practice the compulsion of washing your hands again and again.

Symptoms of obsessive-compulsive disorder usually include compulsions and obsessions. Some symptoms of this disorder can be various obsessions, such as fear of contamination or dirt, and needing things orderly and symmetrical. There are also unwanted thoughts, aggression, or horrific thoughts about losing control, harming yourself or others, and difficulty tolerating uncertainty. OCD usually begins in teens or young adults, but can also start in childhood. The symptoms can become severe throughout life. Obsessions can also change with time, but symptoms generally worsen when a person experiences greater stress. OCD is usually considered a lifelong disorder, it can have mild-to-moderate symptoms, but sometimes the symptoms can be severe and time-consuming, so much so that they become disabling.

OCD can run in families. Having a parent or other family member who suffers from this disorder can increase a person's risk of developing OCD. Stressful life events and traumatic events can also increase a person's risk of developing OCD. Other mental disorders, such as anxiety disorders, depression, substance abuse, and tic disorders can also cause OCD. On a side note, I also made a kick-ass video about the psychosomatic patterns behind OCD (and anxiety) on my YouTube channel evettevideos.com. Just type in the keywords in the search bar.

Separation anxiety

Separation anxiety is characterized by an individual feeling excessive fear when they are separated from a person to whom they are attached. People with separation anxiety fear a lot for the other person's safety. They feel excessive worry about potential harm to this person or losing this person; to whom they feel attached.

During childhood development, separation anxiety is a normal part of it. It occurs in babies between eight and twelve months and normally disappears around the age of two. However, separation anxiety can also occur among adults. The symptoms of separation anxiety in children include clinging to parents, extreme crying, and refusal to do things that require them to be separate from their caregivers. This can also include violent and emotional temper tantrums. It can also include refusal to go to school, poor school performance, nightmares, and refusing to sleep alone.

Children with a family history of anxiety and depression are more likely to develop separation anxiety. A shy and timid personality is also prone to developing separation anxiety. Childhood environments such as overprotective parents can also develop separation anxiety in an individual. If children do not have enough appropriate parental interaction, they can also develop separation anxiety. Stressful events in life can also be a factor risk factor.

Post-traumatic stress disorder

Post-traumatic stress disorder or PTSD is a kind of disorder that develops after a person experiences a traumatic event or witnesses such an event. In post-traumatic stress disorder, a person re-experiences traumatic events in the form of dreams or flashbacks. The person might have difficulty facing situations that remind them of the traumatic event. All these disorders can have different symptoms and causes, but one thing that is common among all is that all of them hinder people from functioning normally in their daily lives. It is especially important to identify if someone is suffering from any kind of anxiety disorder so they can get the right treatment at the right time.

Symptoms of post-traumatic stress disorder include reliving the traumatic experience. It can include having nightmares or flashbacks about the traumatic experience. Post-traumatic stress disorder can also cause people to avoid certain situations which remind them of traumatic events. It also causes a change in beliefs and feelings about other people. You might not trust them anymore. Post-traumatic stress disorder can make you feel that the world is a dangerous place. PTSD also causes hyperarousal. Hyperarousal refers to a state of constantly being on alert. Semantic symptoms, such as physical pain, which cannot be diagnosed, are also an underlying cause of post-traumatic stress disorder.

Causes of post-traumatic stress disorder can include physical, emotional, or sexual abuse, which was in the past or even ongoing. Childhood neglect can also cause post-traumatic stress disorder. Being affected by living in a war zone for a long period or being a prisoner of war can also cause PTSD.

The anxiety spectrum

On the spectrum of anxiety disorders, normal levels of anxiety lies on one end. The low level of anxiety can appear as fear, apprehension, doubts in your skills, and some mild sensations in muscles that can feel as muscle tightness and sweating. It is important to note that normal levels of anxiety do not interfere with daily life activities. They can improve a person's attention span and problem-solving. It can motivate a person to work harder towards achieving a goal. A normal level of anxiety can also warn a person against a potential threat. Normal levels of anxiety can be adaptive and helpful in daily life.

On the other end of the spectrum are the clinical levels of anxiety. Anxiety disorders occur when the levels of anxiety rise high enough to decrease a person's daily life performance and affect daily life activities.

Between these two evident ends of the spectrum, there also lies a gray area in the middle of the spectrum. This is referred to as " almost anxiety". This state occurs when the level of anxiety you feel is not helping you in your daily life performance and is no longer adaptive. It becomes a barrier to daily life enjoyment, but it does not meet the diagnostic threshold for an anxiety disorder.

If you are suffering from almost anxiety, you may feel distracted because of your negative thoughts. It can also cause unpleasant body sensations. It is possible for a person suffering from almost anxiety to sit at their desk all day and make minimal progress on work that is due because they are constantly worried and physically drained. For such a person, the levels of anxiety were not high enough to stop them from coming to work, but they made it difficult for the person to complete the task at hand. If you can recognize almost anxiety, it can help you detect anxiety before it becomes very extreme and diagnostic. Almost anxiety can be targeted using evidence-based strategies.

It is important to tackle almost anxiety because it's harmful to physical and mental health. Experts refer to almost anxiety as a subthreshold condition. This means that the symptoms fall below the level of the required diagnosis of an anxiety disorder. Many studies suggest that subthreshold anxiety is associated with significant life interference. People with subthreshold panic disorder are at an increased risk for other psychiatric disorders, such as depression and substance abuse problems. They also report lower life satisfaction and greater work disability, so it is very important to deal with almost anxiety at an early age so that it does not develop into an anxiety disorder. It is important to pay attention to it so that we can push it back on the spectrum towards low-level anxiety and stop it from reaching the other end of the spectrum.

Treating anxiety as a character flaw

Many people have the misinterpretation that having anxiety disorders is a character flaw. They think it is a problem that happens because the sufferer is weak. But the symptoms of anxiety do not go away, simply by the sufferer deciding for them to go away. Anxiety is not something a person can control, and it is as much a disorder as a heart attack or any other physical disease.

Anxiety disorders are not a sign of character flaws. It is not the fault of the sufferer to be experiencing anxiety. Anxiety disorder is a mood disorder, which affects a person's functionality in daily life.

Anxiety is not a character's fault, and it is nothing to be ashamed of. People need to realize that anxiety and any other mental illness can happen to anyone. It is not a sign of weakness. This is very common for human beings to make false assumptions about things they are not truly aware of. Any person who has suffered from anxiety knows that it is not a character's fault, and if they see another person suffering from a mental disorder, they do not regard that person as weak. But for people who have not experienced anxiety, it's difficult to understand that anxiety is not a character's fault. Such people need to recognize that anxiety is a mood disorder that can happen to anyone, and it is not anyone's fault to be suffering from anxiety.

A person who is suffering from anxiety already has a lot to deal with. They have a lot of negative thoughts along with physical problems. If they have to deal with criticism from people, it does not help them at all. In my personal experience of anxiety, I realized many people judged me for going through that difficult phase of my life. They treated it as if it was my fault to be suffering from anxiety. It made it more difficult for me to deal with my negative thoughts and emotions. Having no external support made it even harder to deal with anxious thoughts and feelings. Therefore, if you have suffered from anxiety, you realize that anxiety is not a character flaw. The point? Don't be an asshole to people suffering from anxiety because they already have enough bullshit to deal with. If people in your life cannot understand this, then unfuck your friendship circle, fire them as friends and get new ones.

Probable Causes of Anxiety

Brain chemicals

Researchers also believe that certain brain chemicals may play a role in causing or worsening anxiety disorders. These brain chemicals are called neurotransmitters and include serotonin, dopamine, gamma-amino-butyric acid (GABA), and norepinephrine.

Another brain chemical that can cause anxiety is norepinephrine. Norepinephrine handles the "fight or flight" response that we feel when we are in danger. This response can cause symptoms such as a racing heart, sweating, and trembling. In people with anxiety disorders, it triggers this response even when there is no real danger present.

Finally, gamma-amino-butyric acid (GABA) is a brain chemical that helps to calm the nervous system. It has linked low levels of GABA to increased anxiety and panic attacks.

Serotonin

One of the most well-known brain chemicals is serotonin. Serotonin is a neurotransmitter that plays a role in mood, social behavior, digestion, and sexual desire. When levels of serotonin are low, it can lead to feelings of anxiety and depression. Diet, exercise, sleep, and medications can affect serotonin levels. Therefore, it's important to pay attention to your overall health if you're trying to manage your anxiety.

Cortisol

Cortisol is another important brain chemical for anxiety. Cortisol is often referred to as the "stress hormone" because it is released in response to stressful situations. When cortisol levels are high, it can lead to an increase in heart rate and blood pressure. This "fight-or-flight" response is meant to help us deal with dangerous situations; however, when we're constantly under stress, cortisol levels can remain elevated, which can lead to anxiety and other health problems.

Dopamine

Dopamine is a neurotransmitter that is involved in motivation, pleasure, and movement. Dopamine is also involved in the "reward circuit" of the brain, which means it plays a role in reinforcement learning—or associating certain behaviors with pleasure or rewards. When dopamine levels are too low, it can lead to feelings of apathy and depression. However, when dopamine levels are too high, it can lead to feelings of mania or hyperactivity. While dopamine isn't directly linked to anxiety, imbalances in dopamine levels can indirectly contribute to anxiety symptoms.

Chapter 2

A brief look at the history of anxiety

Anxiety is as old as woolly mammoths and has been around since humans set foot on the earth. Anxiety has not always been recognized as a mental disorder. It was after several years that anxiety was recognized as a potential medical disorder and a treatable condition. Discovering ways how to treat anxiety even took longer than this. Anxiety is a core part of human evolution, so it has always been there. It was in the era of Greek rule when the term "hysteria" was a diagnosis. They believed that it only affected women. Even the word hysteria has its root in the word "hysteria", which means uterus.

They believed that anxiety or hysteria and behaviors resulting from anxiety, such as panic, were caused by the uterus. The male philosophers of that time believed that hysteria wandered around the body and blocked passages, obstructing breathing, and causing this disease. The renowned philosopher "Plato" also hypothesized this belief. During the early Renaissance, they accused women, in particular, who were highly anxious and prone to the hysteria of being witches and practicing witchcraft. Anxiety makes a person believe bad things are about to happen, so when these women who were suffering from anxiety had premonitions about bad things happening, and if those things came true by chance, then these women were accused of witchcraft.

During ancient times in history, if people were vocal about their anxiety or if they expressed physical symptoms that others could not explain, it led them to be treated via torture in Spain, execution in Britain, and burning at the stake in Scotland.

Even in the Victorian era, the general views about anxiety did not change. Women who got hysterical were crazy. They mainly trapped women indoors. They did not have a job or anything relaxing to do. They had to take care of entire families, bear children, and had much more responsibilities than men. All these conditions led to hysteria among women. If a woman had persistent panic attacks, then her family would cart her off to the local insane asylum, where treatments included electroshock therapy and many other drastic ways.

In the American Civil War, they thought soldiers suffered from what they then knew as "irritable heart syndrome". In this condition, the soldiers exhibited heart palpitations, and they experienced other symptoms of anxiety, such as shortness of breath and sweating. What they experienced was what is now known as post-traumatic stress disorder. When these soldiers exhibited symptoms of post-traumatic stress disorder, they were treated with opium. They established anxiety as a "nerve weakness" in the late 1800s.

During this time, ethyl alcohol and bromide salts were used to treat the symptoms of anxiety. This era also had some benefits regarding the development of anxiety as a medical condition. The general view about anxiety somehow shifted towards a better perspective, as men were now also considered to be suffering from this condition and the gender biases regarding anxiety ended. The treatments that were used during this era of history were only short-term solutions, and they ultimately made the symptoms of anxiety even worse and untreatable. These treatments only gave more discomfort to the patient.

In the early 20th century, the Russians sent psychologists off to war along with soldiers to treat them after a battle. This happened during the Russian war with Japan in 1904. During this period, it was also assumed that anxiety is a condition that could be transferred to children, so sterilization was also used. In the 1930s, they saw a better approach to the treatment of anxiety. During this time, they also introduced some muscle relaxation techniques. Most of the modern techniques for treating anxiety that we are now aware of came into existence after the 1950s.

They also realized that antidepressants could be effective in treating anxiety as they can treat depression as well. The term "anxiety disorder" was first established in the 1980s. They also discovered that antidepressants work on anxiety because anxiety reduces the number of neurotransmitters responsible for bringing happy hormones, such as dopamine and serotonin, to the brain. The history of anxiety is brutal, as it appears that mankind failed to understand anxiety for a long period. People suffering from anxiety were not treated effectively, which could have helped them. Instead, such methods were used, which made their situation even worse. But in the modern era, work on anxiety is being done, and we are trying to understand more about anxiety daily. In our search for answers related to anxiety-related problems, we are also looking back at the history of anxiety for potential cures used during that time.

Triggers of anxiety

It is very important to discover the factors that trigger anxiety because if we are not aware of what triggers our anxiety, then it can become very difficult to deal with it. We might then fight against something and not understand why. Awareness of the causes of anxiety can help you better deal with the symptoms of anxiety. Symptoms of anxiety can be as complicated as marriage.

A combination of factors, including genetics and environmental reasons, can likely be the cause. Research has proven that some emotional events or experiences can cause anxiety. These elements are called triggers of anxiety. For each person, the triggers of anxiety can be different, but some triggers of anxiety can also be common among people. It is also possible that, for some people, anxiety attacks can be triggered in the absence of any triggers. It may appear that these attacks are appearing for no reason at all. Identifying anxiety triggers is an important step in managing anxiety.

Some common anxiety triggers can be:

Health

Health issues can be a trigger of anxiety. And diagnosis that is difficult or upsetting, such as a chronic illness or cancer, can trigger anxiety, and it can also make existing symptoms of anxiety worse. This type of trigger is powerful because it has immediate and personal feelings associated with it. It is possible to reduce anxiety caused by these triggers by being proactive or engaging with a doctor and using self-help tools.

Medications

Some over-the-counter medications can also trigger symptoms of anxiety. That's because some active ingredients in these medications can make people feel uneasy or unwell. These feelings can set off a series of events in the mind and body, which can lead to additional symptoms of anxiety. Some common medications that can trigger anxiety are birth control pills, cough medicines, congestion medicines, and weight loss medicines. These medications can also trigger existing anxieties and worsen their effects. Often the reason for these triggers can show a person their fight or flight response system is on high alert and overstimulated. We will dive more into this shortly.

Caffeine

It is a sad reality that your morning cup of coffee can also be a trigger of anxiety. Many people rely on their morning coffee to wake up, but it triggers anxiety. According to research, drinking about five cups of coffee increases anxiety and induces panic attacks in people with panic disorder. According to another research done about consuming energy drinks, they also showed that energy drinks increase anxiety in males. Therefore, caffeine can be a trigger of anxiety. If you can identify that it triggers your anxiety, then it is important to replace your coffee with a non-caffeinated option. However, different people have different tolerance levels for caffeine. Research has proven that caffeine is an easy trigger to deal with, as simply cutting back from two to three cups of coffee can help people deal with symptoms of anxiety.

Skipping meals

If we skip meals, our blood sugar level drops. It can lead to anxiety deficiency of sugar in blood level and can also lead to jittering hands and other physical effects. It is important to note that food can easily affect our mood. It provides us with energy and important nutrients. So, if we do not make time for three meals a day or healthy snacks, then we can end up feeling nervous or agitated. This can lead to worsening symptoms of anxiety.

Negative thinking

It is well known that the mind and body are not separate entities. Both are correlated and influence the health of the other one. Our mind affects our body, and our body affects our mind. Therefore, negative thinking can trigger anxiety. If we use a lot of negative words when thinking about ourselves, it can also trigger anxiety. It can creep up on you slowly. Even when you have a swift negative thought, it can trigger anxiety. Then, when our anxiety is triggered, it causes us to think negatively, so we are stuck in a loop that may feel impossible to get out of. During my Unfuck Your Life series online course, we dive deep into breaking these patterns.

Social events

For many people, events requiring them to make small talk or interact with people can trigger feelings of anxiety. Being in a room full of strangers can easily trigger social anxiety disorder. A public event such as public speaking, talking in front of your boss, performing in a competition, or reading aloud in a room full of people can also trigger anxiety.

Conflict

Conflicts in relationships can also trigger anxiety. If you identify that conflict in relationships or arguments is acting as a trigger to your anxiety, then you should learn conflict resolution strategies. This can also show that deeper rejection wounds are being triggered by your past.

Personal triggers

Personal triggers can be very difficult to identify because they vary from person to person. It can also be difficult for therapists to identify these triggers, but it is not impossible. Personal triggers can include a place, song, smell, texture, or any other thing. Personal triggers remind a person, consciously or subconsciously, of a negative memory or traumatic event of the past. People who suffer from post-traumatic stress disorder frequently experience personal anxiety triggers. It is very important to identify personal triggers so that we can address them by applying the correct strategic tools. If you experience personal triggers, it can also be easy to deal with them if you stay mindful of them. What helped me to a certain extent was by reminding myself that I am not in the past and the past is not real anymore.

Messy home environment

This is not a trigger of anxiety, which is very clear. Messy home environments don't always cause stress or anxiety among people. However, if a person is suffering from anxiety, then a messy home environment can make an enormous difference. It is important to evaluate your room and home environment. A cluttered home can exasperate anxiety. When you are in a messy environment, your thoughts also become messy, as the environment influences our neural functioning.

It is easier to think more clearly in a clean environment. For some people, organizing things or cleaning activities can also be helpful when they are anxious. Anxiety research has proven that messy home environments can trigger anxiety, and it can cause insomnia, increased stress, inability to focus, and many other adverse effects on health.

Although it is not true for everyone, however, if a messy home environment is an anxiety trigger for you, then by simply clearing away clutter, you can reduce your symptoms. I have also met clients who felt calm in a messy environment as they associated mess and clutter with safety. Why? It reminded their subconscious mind of childhood memories that they found comfort in.

Self-neglect

Self-care can be very difficult, as we are programmed to think more about other people than we think about ourselves. There are very few people in the world who take time out for their own well-being regularly. Neglecting yourself and not taking care of your personal needs can be an anxiety trigger. The mind and body are closely related. If the body is neglected, the mind will also feel the effect of this neglect. It is a common observation that if you're not showering regularly and you're skipping meals or your sleep pattern is disturbed, then you will experience more anxiety than usual.

Disturbed sleep pattern

They link lack of sleep to a lot of mental and physical health issues. They correlated sleep deprivation and anxiety, as one can trigger the other. Sleep deprivation can cause anxiety, and anxiety can, in return, make it difficult for a person to fall asleep by keeping the brain occupied with disturbing thoughts. Minor changes, such as practicing good hygiene and creating a good sleep schedule, can make a lot of difference in the symptoms of anxiety. We will dive more into this shortly.

Stress

This is the most common trigger of anxiety. This is a common part of life, and it can be difficult to avoid stress in the daily hurdles of life. Stress is a very prominent trigger for anxiety. Stress and anxiety can also result in a loop, as stress can trigger anxiety, and anxiety can make it difficult to control stress. There are various ways to reduce stress, but it is important to find the way which works best for you.

Work environment

Work environments can also be a trigger of anxiety. It is normal to deal with occasional stress and anxiety in the work environment, but if it becomes continuous, then it can become a trigger of constant anxiety, and it needs to be addressed. If you associate a place where you spend 70% of your time with anxiety, then you can clearly see how quickly anxiety can become a layered stress response in your mind and nervous system.

Memories of past traumas

Memories of past traumas can also trigger anxiety. If the memories have been suppressed, even then, they can become triggers for anxiety. A certain thing may trigger anxiety, but if we have suppressed the actual memory behind it, then we cannot know what is triggering our anxiety. When we are exposed to environments, situations, or people that bring back unpleasant memories, it can trigger an exaggerated anxiety response.

Negative memories can cause possibly more intense anxiety attacks. The result? More bad memories of the recent panic attacks and the circumstances under which they occurred are also created. This creates an association between memories and anxiety attacks. It increases the odds of more memory-induced attacks in the future. Anxiety can also be reinforced by having an awareness of it, rather than it serving as a signal to deal with it. So, if you fear feeling anxiety and then experience it, it can spiral and worsen anxiety symptoms. Unpleasant memories of past failures or humiliations may sharpen or stimulate awareness.

Environmental changes

People who suffer from anxiety attacks also experience physical sensitivities. These physical sensitivities manifest in alarming ways. People who have a constant possibility of an anxiety attack react to weather changes. They can experience anxiety if the weather differs from how it was earlier in the day or the day before. This also applies to indoor environments. If people who suffer from anxiety go to a different place, it can set off a panic attack. New environments can trigger fear of the unknown, which can then trigger fear of losing control.

These feelings can create uncertainty, and uncertainty can trigger anxiety. Being exposed to new people, along with environmental change, can intensify the anxiety effects. This type of anxiety also deeply affected my quality of life. I felt frozen, and sometimes, I couldn't leave the house for weeks. It was a mindfuck to go from one day leaving the house and then the next, I felt frozen, and everything felt unsafe.

I learned that often triggers of anxiety are most commonly self-generated. The reason for this is that anxiety attacks are a manifestation of an underlying issue. If someone has a history of anxiety attacks, then research proves it is highly likely that deeper emotional or physical problems are also present beneath the surface. If these emotional or psychological problems which are present beneath the surface go undetected and untreated, they manifest themselves as anxiety.

So, anxiety attacks are warning signs of the body or nervous system and a cry for help. If these warning signs are not paid attention to, then it can lead to a lot of suffering and unhappiness and it can make anxiety untreatable and non-diagnosable.

Unfuck Your Anxiety

Chapter 3

Inherited anxiety

Something that people rarely consider while exploring anxiety is that anxiety can be inherited from your parents and throughout the ancestry. This makes perfect sense because anxiety becomes deeply programmed throughout the nervous system, and the nervous system passes its memories down to generations and generations. The primary motive of this is to ensure survival. Imagine your nervous system is like the black box in an airplane. These black boxes in airplanes capture all data until the moment the airplane crashes. Your nervous system metaphorically functions the same way.

However, a lot of information that the nervous system has captured is passed down to offspring, and their information is added along with the pre-existing information that is being recorded and so forth. This is great news and a very much more complex way of dissecting and understanding anxiety. What that means is that anxiety does not start with you. It can start from your ancestry and be triggered in your life. When we look at how the nervous system is wired, its purpose is to help regulate the body and to help send messages and signals back and forth so that your body can function in its optimal way.

Anxiety programmed during your development

There are a lot of patterns when we address anxiety. There is some powerful evidence of anxiety being inherited from a parent. In most cases, not all we inherit is from the mother. Why? Even though you spent nine months of your developmental stages in the womb, there is a lot more to this than just this basic understanding. A lot of the mother's emotions, fears, and thoughts can have a tremendous influence on the child's emotional well-being, health, organ development, and even brain development.

It can also influence the unborn child's nervous system and how it responds to his or her environment after birth. The more stress, fear, and anxiety the mother experienced during her pregnancy, the more heightened the child's sensitivity is to stress. Many of my students and clients reported accurate memories and powerful emotions that their mothers also experienced during their fetal developmental stages. What does this tell you? That there is a strong possibility that there could be certain thoughts and emotions that you express that didn't start with you. However, how would you know the difference? That's the tough part because these emotions and sensations have been with you from the day that you were born.

Therefore, we accept what has already been present since the day we were born. One of many reasons for this is that in the past, the placenta was a barrier between the mother and the child, protecting the child from the chemicals and stress of the mother. This has been blown out of the water quite some time ago.

Cortisol, which is a stress response hormone released by the mother's body in a state of distress, is toxic for a developing child. So, what that means is the more stressed the mother was during her pregnancy and the more cortisol her body released, the more it could have negatively influenced developmental stages. A developing fetus's body cannot deal with a tremendous amount of cortisol released by the mother's body. It is a known fact (not just an Evette fact) that cortisol can penetrate through the placenta and influence the development of the child.

Why is this so fundamental? Remember that your placenta is the startup of your being. If your placenta is not healthy and functioning optimally, then that will reflect on your psychological and physical health. So, if you have tremendous challenges with anxiety, have a conversation with your mother and ask her what her experience with her pregnancy was.

If your developmental stages are filled with anxiety and fear, it is bound to influence the cellular development of your brain, organs, and psychological development.

Let us look at the technical side and check out the research behind this.

"If we can understand the mechanisms by which prenatal stress programs the developing brain, we may short-circuit or even prevent this programming and help a child survive and thrive," says Prof. Eero Castrén of the University of Helsinki's Faculty of Biological Sciences, who led the research. [1]

In their experiment, scientists from Helsinki have been studying molecules that help transmit signals from the sensory system to other parts of the central nervous system, in particular a molecule called substance P. In stressful situations, substance P triggers an internal signaling cascade within neurons whose result is a release of glucocorticoids via a signaling pathway called MAPK/ERK. This cascade was already known to play a key role in the development of neuronal circuits, but its ability to induce epigenetic changes that would be permanent and carried into adulthood was not known before.

Between April and October 2011, a team from the Institute Universitaire de Médecine Sociale et Préventive in Lausanne examined the extent to which glucocorticoids affect brain development by studying populations of pregnant women who had either been diagnosed with a psychiatric disorder or had been downsized from jobs. To examine whether glucocorticoids affected fetal brain development, researchers collected umbilical cord blood samples from 27 pairs of mothers and their children while they were still in the hospital following childbirth. The male babies in this sample population averaged a gestational age of 38 weeks, while the female babies averaged 37 weeks gestation.

Besides looking at glucocorticoid levels, researchers measured cortisol levels in the 27 umbilical cord blood samples. This helped them to determine whether cortisol, a less potent stress hormone than glucocorticoid, might also affect fetal brain development.

Effects of prenatal stress, such as fear or anxiety, can be seen at different endocrine levels (neuroendocrine). Elevated maternal cortisol levels will increase blood flow through the uterus and cervix, stimulating contractions. This results in premature birth or spontaneous abortion. As a result, prenatal stress reduces adult hippocampal neurogenesis (cell proliferation), providing direct evidence of its impact on brain development."

"As early as the second trimester of pregnancy, children who later develop autism show decreased eye fixation relative to typically developing children when they are shown an image of a real face."

"Prenatal stress effects can be seen in social behavior and cause long-term alterations to the HPA axis, even after infancy. These changes that take place during early development have been suggested to lead to lifelong problems with mood regulation."

The results of this study help us better understand how prenatal stress affects fetal brain development. The researchers found that high levels of maternal glucocorticoids are associated with smaller hippocampal volumes in children. Moreover, lower maternal cortisol levels are associated with decreased risk for psychiatric disorders later in life despite prenatal exposure to stress hormones.

There is a significant difference between groups detected at all times except gestational weeks 32 and 36. The significant difference between the high-stress (HS) group and the control (C) group was detected at gestational week 28, at which point there were significantly lower left hippocampal volumes in children of stressed mothers. This result shows that prenatal stress may affect fetal brain development negatively because glucocorticoids are associated with smaller hippocampal volume despite exposure to just cortisol alone. However, the negative effects of prenatal stress do not take effect until later in childhood.

The researchers are currently investigating whether this finding means that if a child is exposed to both glucocorticoids and cortisol prenatally, they should have an increased risk for psychiatric disorders.

People who experience chronic stress are at risk of developing health problems. Stress can contribute to various cardiovascular diseases, suppress the immune system, and increase the risk of diabetes and osteoporosis.

Environmental or prenatal stress can affect a child's future development. This is especially true for children born to women who experienced stressful events during their pregnancy. A growing body of research suggests that these children may suffer from mood disorders in later life and have an elevated risk of obesity. However, it is important to note that not all studies found such associations, so we need more research before we decide whether stress in utero can cause different types of harm.

One-way prenatal stress affects the fetus is by activating a mediator in pregnant women called cortisol. Cortisol is a hormone that your body produces to help you cope with stress. It increases blood sugar levels and suppresses the immune system.

The developing fetus needs to have cortisol in its mother's bloodstream because it signals the placenta to divert energy resources away from other tasks, such as growth, towards processes related to dealing with stress. This study by Maeda et al. investigates whether prenatal stress can change how much cortisol crosses the placenta and therefore alter fetal development [1].

Cortisol has been widely researched and can have a big impact on a developing fetus. Cortisol is a steroid hormone produced in humans by the adrenal glands at the top of the kidneys in response to stress. Researchers want to understand cortisol's role in treating psychiatric disorders.

Cortisol belongs to a family of hormones called glucocorticoids which increase glucose levels via carbohydrate metabolism, suppress the immune system, reduce bone formation, alter salt retention, promote fat breakdown (i.e., mobilization) and induce protein catabolism which results in amino acid uptake by cells' mitochondria for the production inside them.

A study published in the "Journal of Child Psychology and Psychiatry" examined cortisol levels in 65 pregnant women. They found that higher maternal cortisol levels during pregnancy were associated with increased stress reactions in the umbilical artery shortly after birth, lower scores on motor examinations two weeks later, and poorer motor coordination by age 6. The pattern of chronic anxiety has also been reported.

Copied anxiety

Being a parent is damn hard. It's probably one of the hardest tasks that you will ever tackle in your life if you are not already a parent, and you choose to become one. If you are one, you will know exactly what I'm talking about right now, and you are probably anxious due to sleep deprivation as well.

Being a parent is difficult because you have to take care of another human being entirely. If you are a mother, you may not have recovered fully from the effects of pregnancy and delivery when you are handed a human being. A child depends on you for everything. You are completely unaware of how to tackle this situation if it is your first time. Even if it is not your first time, it is still difficult as the needs of every child differ from the other one.

Being a parent can bring on tremendous amounts of anxiety, especially when you feel out of your depth and unresourceful concerning the child and behavioral patterns that they might have. You might also have struggled with anxiety before you had children. Regardless of where you are on the scale, it is a known fact that a child can copy a parent's behavior. This is a powerful statement to make and one that is true. As children mature, they mimic and copy their parents' behavioral patterns. A child will also copy a parent's coping strategies. A child will also take notice of how a parent deals with certain stressful factors. Why? Parents are a child's role model, and you even see this inherited trait in animals as they copy their parent's hunting skills for food and so forth.

This is a survival skill that is naturally inbred into all of us. These skills serve as a powerful platform for learning and understanding how to act and behave in life when a youngster has no prior knowledge. This wonderful experience and pattern of copying are powerful. It leaves a lasting result that can propel a child forward into powerful adult life. However, in this case, it could also take a turn for the worst when the child copies a parent who is struggling in life.

Here is a moment where a child can go two ways. The option is the child can copy the parents' anxious and worrying traits. The other option is if the child is born with a certain resiliency toward stressful circumstances that have been inherited.

Children are often thrown into an adult role very early in their life. They might end up taking the parent role. From a very young and immature age, they had to problem-solve and deal with complicated circumstances and emotions with no stable guidance. The child can have one anxious parent and another more stable parent. This can help the child see a reference and a difference in relation to how to deal with stress. Helpful support can also come as having supportive teachers or mentors that can serve as a healthy, stable reference point for the child to learn from.

That includes how to deal with stress. Sometimes very basic skills are absent when parenting a child. A good example is when a person becomes enraged, upset, sad, or feels out of control of a situation. How they react to that situation can leave a lasting impression on the child and how they think they should cope with similar circumstances.

In a perfect world, the ideal method would be to apply a calm way to handle powerful emotions and stressful circumstances. Why? Then the child can copy that same approach to a problem.

To see a problem and feel in control rather than seeing a problem and feeling out of control. Another important absent factor is for a child to learn to understand what emotions are and how to express them. Surely you know what it feels like when you have heavy emotions that are laying like stones in your heart, and you can't talk about it.

The worst part is not knowing how to articulate even what you feel because maybe during your childhood, you were never taught this art of learning to understand your emotions. Maybe your emotions were rejected or punished. If that is the case, we form negative associations with our emotions. So, when our emotions come up, we suppress them. However, the body has a threshold like anything else in life does.

The body can only hold on to so much emotional stress until the body speaks to you as anxiety, tension, or headaches, to let you know something is suppressed. These messages need to be released. However, imagine now that you have this negative association with expressing yourself and your emotions. Can you do the math of the outcome?

Chapter 4

Dealing with anxiety in life

When you feel anxious and unsafe about your environment, you might feel more hypervigilant in relation to your safety. You might worry if your doors and windows are locked properly.

There must have been a time when you left your house and felt your heart racing, thinking, "shit, did I lock the door?" You are having negative thoughts towards yourself, "why was I not more careful or double-checked everything," and then the anxiety kicks in. It can sometimes often feel like your body is flooded with cortisol, propelling you to take action to go back to the house to check the door and windows. It is hard to switch off this anxiety and stress response, especially if it triggers a prior old memory associated with a time when someone might have broken into your house.

Two experiences take place, and one is when you feel the physical sensations and response of your body and then the other aspect is all the thoughts that surface with it as well.

The thought was whether you locked the door, scrambled through memories, or recalculated your steps and moves before you left the house. The reason is that we have two separate pathways that allow for anxiety to be communicated and felt.

Prior memories come forward of times when the house was broken into versus another part of the brain where anxiety can be traveling from, which is called the amygdala. This part of the brain is called our panic button because it has the knee-jerk reaction and immaturity of a four-year-old child. You have seen how irrational children often can be. The amygdala is the same. However, at that moment, you're also trying to calm yourself by saying everything is ok.

You are constantly assuring yourself that you locked the door, and then you think of solutions like calling the neighbor to check and so forth. Here, you are using a mindfulness practice tool and taking action toward a solution part rather than exasperating the problem part. This can help you drastically decrease your anxiety tremendously. What's happening at this moment is that your frontal cortex is supporting and soothing your amygdala by also, in conjunction, stimulating the hippocampus. The hippocampus is the emotional brain that revives memories associated with solutions you are trying to establish.

Let's break this down even more because this example is here to serve as a simpler way of explaining how anxiety can manifest. When you realized you might not have locked the door, you felt panicked, and then you felt anxious. Your thoughts were racing, a lot of images were coming forward of fears that were projected, and fears connected to actual events from the past from prior memories when someone broke into the house.

It triggered different parts of your brain, including your nervous system. You must have felt your body tremble slightly. The reason for this is the body is experiencing a biochemical response of an older memory, which is now activated. What is the memory? It could relate to invasion trauma or a memory when something was taken from you when you were careless or off guard.

The reason your body is also trembling is that adrenaline and cortisol are being released. It also triggered the flight and fight response when we felt anxious. It then releases cortisol throughout the body. This survival coping strategy in our biological makeup helped and saved our ancestors in the past from danger. When they experience a threat cortisol, and adrenaline are released, giving them enough energy, confidence, and stamina to take action, move or run. We still have this same survival response running through our veins.

However, what do we do when we become stressed? We have new coping mechanisms that involve everything but running or physical movement that could help the body discharge cortisol. Where do you think this cortisol is going? It's not being used for the purpose that it is designed for. This cortisol floods the body and the nervous system with messages of urgency and distress. The body understands that it needs to do something. However, it cannot detect anything in its immediate environment that would validate to the body why it feels the way it does. This is the biggest mind-fuck of anxiety.

So, what is happening right now is that you are responding to a valid fear that you have. However, your body is also triggering prior fears, traumas, or thoughts that you have. This may not always be the case. In most cases, what we're experiencing is what is called a split duality. That means when you feel anxiety, it is because you're feeling it in the present moment. However, in most cases, this anxiety is triggered by prior traumas and subconscious memories in the past.

Anything can trigger anxiety. There is no need for it to be an actual event. It can be the voice of a person, smell, color, or a certain sound. It also depends on your emotional state. You must have noticed that there are days when you feel more anxious than others. The reason for that is you might have noticed on the days when you felt less anxious that you might have felt calm, less vulnerable, or confident.

Whereas on the days when you felt very anxious that morning when you woke up, you might have already gotten out of bed on the wrong side, and you felt upset and vulnerable because of perhaps dreams that triggered certain states of consciousness in you. For example, you might also have had a bad day and you still feel down the next day.

Let's go to the explanation of what happened when you forgot to lock the door. So, your mind is having a reaction to anxiety along with memories being triggered and cortisol flooding your body. It will add more stress to your autonomic nervous system. The autonomic nervous system is connected to the nervous system and also supports certain muscles in the body that are connected to our fight-or-flight response to act in moments of threat. That is why when you hear a sudden loud sound that you did not expect, you jump, or you hunch over. Have you noticed how this happens without even thinking about it?

You had no control over it. Here, the muscle responses which are completely automatic are being referred to. We all have different defaults in terms of how we react in a moment of panic. In most cases, when a front door is not locked, people want to run. They want to run back to the house as fast as they can to make sure that everything is ok.

They may even visualize the thought of running. It floods their body with cortisol so much that they tremble. They feel such a powerful urge and need to run to release cortisol. It also supports and motivates them to take action to go back to the house. As explained earlier, the downside of this inherited response from our ancestors is that we do not act and react appropriately to our body when it is stressed.

Releasing this nervous energy can sometimes be simple. You can sprint fast, run the energy out of your body, or even just jump up and down on the spot. These strategies would be ideal for your body. However, how do we handle this type of anxiety? You may sit down and have a glass of wine to find immediate relief from anxiety. However, this now begs the question, "what happens to the cortisol?" Did you apply the correct solution to the immediate problem that you had? Did you apply the correct solution to what your body needed at that moment? The answer to both questions is no. In moments like these, we locked in trauma and anxiety. The body does not adequately release cortisol.

Your body is like glass; it can only handle and take so much until it pours over. What is being referred to here is a panic attack or a meltdown. The reason being the body feels tremendously unresourceful and unable to achieve its natural, harmonious state of calmness. The body is overstimulated, and there's too much cortisol in the body. What happens? The body cannot regulate itself back into a balanced state. That is why we have a panic attack. It's the body's way of trying to push emotions forward and out so we can release them. You can see a panic attack as an emergency self-regulation of your body.

Returning to the example of the door not being locked. Research has shown that the body stores not only memories cognitively, however, it can also store memories throughout the body. Many people are not aware of this because they are used to not feeling their emotions. After all, we have set up our lives to avoid feeling. We are masters at deflecting, and that includes deflecting away from our emotions.

We must understand our bodies to help us deal better with our anxious responses. For example, when you feel unsafe, your leg might feel numb. When you feel anxious, your heart may beat fast, or you feel a prickly sensation in your hands. When you feel sad, your stomach may feel heavy, and your heart also feels heavy. This is called a psychosomatic response to our emotions in the body. When you feel an emotion, it can send signals throughout your entire body. That is why when you feel certain emotions, you might have noticed that certain parts of your body flare up.

You might have noticed when your anxiety feels triggered in certain areas of your body, you feel tension, pain, irritation, and aggravation in the body when you feel anxious. That is because every time you feel an emotion triggered by an anxious moment, that emotion can become memorized and layered into that part of your body. It becomes part of your cognitive memory. So, in the mentioned example, you felt the anxiety. You had flashes of recent memories of the day. It released cortisol. You had such a strong desire to run. However, when you tried to run, your legs felt numb, and perhaps multiple memories were triggered. It then triggered multiple sensations connected to distinct memories at the same time.

That is why your body responded to how it did. This theory is absolutely fascinating, and it has been a huge part of my psychosomatic research for over 15 years. That is also why the book Metaphysical Anatomy Volume one, three and Unfuck Your Trauma was written. Metaphysical Anatomy Volume one is about psychosomatic stress for 679 medical ailments for adults and also children. I will discuss this concept in great detail. Emotions play a big role in relation to how we feel. Emotions and anxiety can exasperate certain ailments that can come forward because of chronic stress.

The biggest problem that we have in life is that we apply the wrong solution to the wrong problem. That means you will not get the outcome that you are searching for. You might end up exasperating it. Or you might end up creating an additional problem on top of your existing problem. Why? The solution method being used is not in alignment with what you truly need to have the desired outcome.

Anxiety is unidentified fear

Anxiety results from old, accumulated fear, panic, and having lost control of your life. Any kind of situation can trigger anxiety. Normally circumstances, where you felt you lost control in the past, could be key trigger points for this type of anxiety to surface. This type of anxiety can also be related to an inherited ancestral trauma.

Anxiety is mostly focused on an identified source. However, anxiety can also be caused because of unidentified fear. It is difficult to identify the original cause of anxiety. Therefore, we can easily assume places, people, or circumstances triggered that anxiety, whereas the actual root cause of the anxiety can be because of something completely different.

It can be overwhelming for people and cause them to shut down, become emotionally withdrawn, and disconnect from people. This includes stopping doing things and activities that they once enjoyed. All because anxiety is associated with people or circumstances that might not be the actual cause of a person's anxiety.

There can be remarkably diverse reasons for the causes of anxiety. Anxiety can be caused by brain chemistry, stress, environmental factors, or traumatic events. It is easy to identify the triggers of anxiety, but identifying the source is a challenging task. A trigger is an event that provokes an anxious response in people suffering from an anxiety disorder rather than being the root cause of why anxiety exists.

It is quite common to feel anxious without being aware of the reason. Many people who feel anxiety feel as if they are feeling distressed for no reason at all. Even if people identify a reason, it is usually vague and bizarre which is a symptom more than a cause. It is very much possible to feel that anxiety comes out of nowhere. It is possible that everything in a person's life is going absolutely fine, but they still experience anxiety. The reason for this is that anxiety comes up because of unidentified fears. Anxiety does not surface without a reason. There is always a cause. It's difficult to identify this cause, but the first step is just to understand that anxiety can be caused by an unidentified reason.

An evolutionary trait of human beings is that they try to forget situations that cause them distress. It is a type of coping mechanism in which a person forgets situations that caused them distress. We also know these coping strategies as suppression and repression. Both are remarkably similar defense mechanisms; people use them in order to cope with inconvenient situations.

"Suppression" is a defense mechanism in which people force themselves to forget unwanted thoughts. This action is conscious and voluntary. Suppression is when a person chooses not to give conscious thought to a feeling, even if they are aware of it. It is very common to suppress emotions when we feel like we cannot deal with them.

On the other hand, "repression," which is also called dissociative amnesia, is the subconscious forgetting of unpleasant thoughts and feelings. Repression causes a person to have no recollection of the sufferings that were experienced during childhood. Although these defense mechanisms are helpful in the short run because people do not have to deal with unpleasant memories. However, memories that are suppressed or repressed manifest later in bigger problems that are more difficult to deal with. These forgotten memories influence our behaviors, and they can also appear as anxiety. In this case, people would not be aware of the true cause, as they no longer remember these suppressed or repressed feelings. So, people end up forgetting the reasons which are causing them distress, but when their effects bubble up as anxiety, they find themselves in a place where they cannot identify the source of their problems and fears anymore.

We can somehow link anxiety to evolution because, as human beings evolved, they developed a response to fight danger known as the "flight or fight" response. The sympathetic nervous system handles this instinctual response. The fight-or-flight response is an automatic psychological reaction to events that are perceived as stressful or frightening. When the sympathetic nervous system perceives a threat, it triggers the acute stress response, which prepares the body to fight or flee. This response is a survival technique that we had to develop in order to evolve. The fight-or-flight response also results in a chain of events that results in physical effects like increased heart rate, increased respiration rate, dilation of pupils, and the skin becoming pale or flushed.

Whenever we experience danger, we might choose to run, or we can choose to fight.

The third response can be to freeze in such a situation. Anxiety or fear developed as a lifesaving action. Sometimes we experience situations that are not life-threatening, but our sympathetic nervous systems are not aware of that, and they treat it as a life-threatening situation. So, we treat these situations with anxiety because the brain activates our fight-or-flight response.

It can also be hard to identify the hidden fears which are causing anxiety because anxiety causes people to feel confused. Because of this confusion and brain fogginess, it becomes difficult to think, and people cannot identify the cause behind their disrupted feelings.

Anxiety can limit how we experience our emotions and how we experience life. I mention emotions here because anxiety can cause a person to feel that all their emotions are negative and bad. The beauty of emotions is that it allows us to fall in love, laugh, and see the good things in life. However, when you are always stuck in a place of pain and distress, that is all that you see and that is what your world becomes. It can affect a person's health. For example, certain foods, such as bread, can bloat you when you're stressed. However, when you are happy, and you eat bread, then your stomach might not react at all.

When you feel anxious and stressed, you may have headaches, whereas when you're happy, you never have headaches. You also must have noticed that when you feel anxiety for long periods of time, you can come down with some sickness, such as the flu. Whereas when things in your life are going well, the flu bug, for instance, would never affect you. Sometimes, even if your entire family is sick, you won't get sick because you are in a good and happy place in your life. Anxiety can be so debilitating that it can rob and influence a person from having powerful experiences in their life. This can, for example, include applying for that perfect job, chasing after that perfect partner, and finding the confidence to create a life that you really, truly want.

Anxiety and phobias

Did you know that most phobias, for example, are related to your ancestry? They are, in most cases, not even from your lifetime. When you observe this type of anxiety, then you are looking at an issue that you feel challenged with, combined with the trauma associated with losing control. Let me explain. For example, let's say you have a fear of heights because you fell from a certain height. Here, falling triggers huge stress and shock because when you fall, you are completely out of control.

Loss of control is one of the worst traumas that the body and mind can experience because losing control on a cellular level (meaning on a biological level) might lead to your death, and it is the body's job to keep you alive. Remember that your body and your mind have unique experiences. Your body sees the world from a fight-or-flight response. Your mind can rationalize information that your body interprets in a more sensible way. So, when you experience this kind of trauma, the body makes sure that it remembers this trauma and triggers sensations from your subconscious mind about how you felt when you lost control while you fell. The intention for this?

To keep you away from any areas that are placed at a high level, intending to keep you alive. The feeling can be intense, and you almost don't have a choice other than to surrender to the fear that you feel. What is interesting about the fear of heights and the anxiety is that you might not have a conscious, clear memory of falling from a prominent place. Remember, this example can apply to many other intense fears, phobias, and anxiety you have. It's not just excluded from heights.

If you specifically have a fear of heights, then three things could be possible. You either fell from a prominent place when you were very young, or your mum could have dropped you by accident. You might not remember; however, your subconscious memory and nervous system do.

Remember that your instinctive responses are firing off well before you develop your hippocampus (emotional brain and a part of your long-term memory). It can also relate to when your mother was pregnant with you, and she fell, causing her shock and trauma to be carried over into your emotional body because of cortisol being released. Then last but not least, you could even have an ancestral memory triggered when an ancestor survived falling from a prominent place. These are just to give a few examples of how anxiety can be stored, triggered, and expressed. All of this is being shared with you so that we can plant a seed of discovery and curiosity deep in your subconscious mind.

It's through curiosity that we have our biggest breakthroughs. This type of anxiety can also include, for example, fear of being in an elevator, or somewhere in public, and severe stress associated with what others think of you. So, the causes of anxiety can be endless, but it doesn't mean that your road to healing has to be endless.

Chapter 5

Signs of anxiety and possible deeper meanings

You have difficulty concentrating

This often happens because your emotions distract you. It can also flip the other way as what I would call in Metaphysical Anatomy Technique the numbness state, which I also refer to in my modality as an instinctive reaction. This is not necessarily something that you would find in research material or psychology data. It comes from observing thousands of people. This state often becomes activated due to long-term stress that has taken a toll on the body, which can also result in depression or trauma. I have also observed that this state can be with a person from the moment they are born.

Some people find it difficult to focus for longer periods, naturally. It does not mean that every time a person has difficulty concentrating is because of anxiety. A short concentration span is not always caused by anxiety, but it can also be a symptom of anxiety. If someone is so affected by their thoughts they cannot concentrate on the present, it can be a sign of anxiety. If a person is constantly worried about a situation, then they won't be able to focus on daily life. This proves that anxiety can affect the concentration span of people.

It is a daily life observation that if the mind is occupied with negative thoughts, then it is difficult to concentrate on things that require attention. This can even include trivial things which require little attention, like boiling a pan of water. Anxiety can cause the mind to be constantly preoccupied with negative thoughts. If the mind is busy dealing with these energy-consuming thoughts, then it is difficult to concentrate on other activities.

I have also noticed that when I am facing a difficult situation, I find it very difficult to concentrate on daily life activities. It affects all areas of my life. Anxiety can make even simple and trivial tasks like brushing teeth or making tea appear frustrating. When I feel better mentally and emotionally, I can focus better on different activities, which also means my concentration span increases significantly.

Anxiety affects an individual's cognitive functioning, which can cause an inability to focus on work. Anxiety and the inability to focus on work are interconnected when a person feels anxious. The mind struggles to perform a task. Anxiety also affects short-term memory functions, which makes it difficult to remember tasks and projects which are due, and it causes more anxious feelings and worries.

Mental confusion, forgetfulness, difficulty concentrating, and foggy thinking are also symptoms of anxiety. Anxiety causes stress hormones to elevate, such as cortisol and adrenaline, and increased level of these hormones causes brain fogginess. The stress hormones also negatively affect cognitive functioning, such as the inability to focus and short-term memory loss. Lack of focus is a common symptom of anxiety disorder.

It is possible to deal with anxiety and the inability to focus on work. The first step would be to understand how anxiety affects cognitive functioning. It is important to understand that you will have to make some adjustments to your habits to increase your focus span. Some steps that can cause increased focus are to take brief breaks. Instead of attempting to complete the task at once, if you try to complete a task in one go, it causes wandering attention and loss of interest.

However, if you break the task into smaller segments and take brief breaks in between, then it increases the attention span by making the brain more relaxed and allowing it to concentrate. If your anxiety is making it difficult to focus on work, and you feel you forget a lot of deadlines, then an easy way should be to maintain a to-do list. At the beginning of each day, take out some time to make a list of all the things that should be completed during the day. This simple approach gave me structure and lessened my anxiety due to work pressure. I always listed the first three most important tasks first, and then when they were marked off, then I knew I was on target.

Also, add free slots to your day so that you do not experience burnout. Try to train yourself to practice mindfulness. Being mindful of the present helps improve focus and concentration on the task at hand. If you feel that your mind has wandered, then take a moment to bring it back to its present and stay mindful of it. If you think you are losing your concentration on a task, then an easy way to regain your attention can be to switch to a different task. This will cause your attention to alternate between the tasks, and it can stimulate better concentration. This also helped me. I would often write three books at the same time to avoid losing concentration and boredom.

Anxiety causes a person to worry excessively about things. You might worry about things that are not even in your control. If you feel you are worried about something, ask yourself this question: "can I do something about it?" If the answer is no, then try to divert your mind from the thought and bring it back to the task at hand.

You avoid social gatherings (engaging with people)

Social anxiety is also known as social phobia. This fear is long-term and overwhelming. People suffering from social anxiety disorder have difficulty talking with people, meeting new people, or attending any kind of social gathering. They feel that other people are judging them, and their actions and moves are being scrutinized and judged. For some people so, social anxiety goes away as they get older.

With time they start getting more comfortable with social gatherings. It is common to confuse social anxiety with shyness. But social anxiety is a fear that does not go away and affects everyday life. Some people occasionally worry about social gatherings as it can be possible that they do not enjoy being in the company of other people or they are just generally introverts. But the difference between such people and people with social anxiety is that people suffering from social anxiety have an overwhelming fear.

Shyness can also affect a person's ability to socialize. But shyness does not disrupt life activities to such an extent as social anxiety does. Social anxiety is overwhelming and does not go away on its own. Social anxiety can be identified if you worry about everyday activities such as starting conversations, meeting with strangers, going to work, going frapping, speaking on the phone, and other daily life activities. You might avoid social activities like group conversations. You might find it difficult to do things when you feel that other people are watching you. You feel that you are being criticized, you have low self-esteem, and you avoid eye contact. People who are suffering from social anxiety also have physical symptoms when their fear is stimulated. You might feel sick; you might feel that your heartbeat is pounding, or you are sweating or trembling. It is also possible for people suffering from social anxiety to experience panic attacks when they are afraid of social gatherings.

It can also cause people to feel that their minds are going blank. Social anxiety can cause nausea, rigid body stance, and difficulty speaking. The psychological symptoms of social anxiety are that people suffer from uncomfortable thoughts very intensely before, during, and after social gatherings. They try to avoid social gatherings, and if they have to attend, they try to hide in the background and not interact with people. Social anxiety causes people to become self-conscious and might also miss their work or avoid attending school because of this anxiety. People suffering from social anxiety disorder avoid all kinds of social situations, whether it is a job interview, shopping, using a public restroom, talking on the phone, eating in public, or simply being asked a question.

It is also possible for people to have limited or selective anxiety. Limited or selected anxiety means that people can have some symptoms of social anxiety disorder, and it is possible that a few things can trigger their anxiety. For example, people with selective anxiety may feel anxious if asked the question, but they do not avoid social gatherings.

So, when you think about attending social gatherings, you might feel vulnerable or unsafe, your defense mechanisms do not feel strong. Your confidence levels do not feel as strong either. This experience might even trigger the fight-or-flight response. This triggers instinctive responses, and one of them, in this case, might be the hide instinct. Why the hide response? Because avoidance in my research can come forward in forms such as isolating yourself. You isolate yourself from potential danger or from potential circumstances that could cause you to feel anxious. You may also avoid feeling old unpleasant emotions and memories from past events that are related to stressful social gatherings. In most cases, it is most likely you had a traumatic event take place with people around you.

It could've been in your family dynamics or associated groups of people with whom you formed negative associations. In cases like these, your subconscious mind is stimulated when it observes a group of people. It gives feedback to the brain to look for similar memories associated with social gatherings so that you can relate to them. So, what happens? It triggers unpleasant memories of moments you had with groups of people. You might not have a conscious recollection of these memories, however, biochemically, your body is reacting to them, and you feel old emotions resurfacing. Experiences from the past come back to life in the blink of an eye.

It is possible to overcome social anxiety by following some tips and tricks. You can start by trying to understand more about your anxiety. It can help to write down what you are thinking and what is going through your mind. You can also analyze how you behave in certain social situations and keep a diary. Trying some meditation or relaxing techniques can also help, such as breathing exercises, before going out. You should not think of dealing with this challenging situation as one big problem. Instead, break it down into small chunks and try to accomplish one thing at a time. This will help you feel more relaxed as you accomplish smaller goals. If you feel you are being judged or criticized, then try to focus on what you are doing right and screw the judgmental fucktarts. People who are suffering from social anxiety understand that their fears are irrational, but they feel powerless over them and cannot do anything to control their fears. This also means it gives no one the right to judge you because of it.

Social anxiety is not something that is only affecting adults. Children can also suffer from it. If a child cries or gets upset more often than usual, then there is a possibility that they might suffer from social anxiety. Children who suffer from social anxiety get angry a lot when interacting with other kids and adults. Children suffering from social anxiety have an intense fear of going to school, taking part in classroom activities or performances at social events. They might not ask for help at school and are emotionally reliant on their parents or caretakers.

It is not exactly known what causes social anxiety disorder, but it results from a combination of factors. These factors can be biological, physical, and genetic. Problems with neurotransmitter systems, which cause imbalances of hormones like serotonin, dopamine, and glutamate, can also cause it. These hormones are important in regulating mood, and their imbalance can cause various problems. Environmental factors can also cause social anxiety. However, it occurs as part of a complex interaction between biological and genetic factors. Emotional, physical, or any other abuse can also result in social anxiety disorder. Over-controlling parenting styles can cause children to develop a social anxiety disorder. It can also be caused because of insecure attachment style. Whatever the cause is, there is a possibility of overcoming it.

You struggle to sleep well at night

Sleep anxiety is a feeling of fear or distress when trying to fall asleep and staying asleep. Anxiety and sleep problems are closely related. Sleep problems can make anxiety worse, and anxiety can make sleep problems worse. So, this creates a never-ending cycle. Stress and anxiety cause our bodies to release hormones that activate our flight-or-fight response. These stress hormones cause the body to constantly stay in "escape mode".

Chronically, high levels of stress hormones can make it difficult for the body to relax and make it difficult for a person to fall asleep. You might have difficulty falling asleep, and if you fall asleep, then you may wake up during the night with troublesome thoughts and may not sleep again. Hypothyroidism is also a condition that is a combination of anxiety and insomnia. It is caused when there is not enough thyroid hormone in our bloodstream, and the metabolism slows down. Research also suggests that anxiety can affect rapid eye movement sleep. It is a phase of sleep in which you have vivid dreams.

A person suffering from anxiety may have disturbing nightmares, which can make it difficult for them to fall or stay asleep. Sleep problems and anxiety are interwoven. In sleep anxiety, a person worries about poor sleep during the day and evening. Stress hormones released from this worry or anxiety can cause poor sleep. Some people may also suffer from nocturnal panic attacks. They happen only at night, often waking you up from sleep. It causes an intense, sudden burst of extreme fear.

Sleep anxiety can affect adults, teens, and children as well. A person will probably develop sleep anxiety if they suffer from insomnia, sleepwalking, sleep apnea, narcolepsy, and restless legs syndrome. People who are suffering from mental health disorders such as depression, bipolar disorder, panic disorder, post-traumatic stress disorder, schizophrenia, and drug addiction can also develop sleep anxiety. Research suggests that most people who suffer from a mental health disorder such as anxiety also suffer from sleep disruption.

If you cannot sleep at night because of anxiety, then you might experience behavioral changes such as feeling overwhelmed, inability to concentrate, nervousness, irritability, and restlessness. Sleep anxiety can also have various physical effects, such as a fast heart rate, sweating, trembling, tense muscles, rapid breathing, and digestive problems.

Sleep anxiety affects many people, and it can disrupt the normal functioning and routine of a person.

From my research and observations, I learned that this is also because the body has several instinctive responses activated throughout the day. The body has not discharged cortisol and stress from the day, which means the body has not regulated itself. I will discuss this in more detail during the next few chapters.

One anxious event can trigger another anxious event. We can spiral into this conundrum if we don't find effective ways to relieve anxiety. That means the body can become stuck, feeling defensive and vulnerable. When we feel defensive, it also means that the body is on high alert. High alert to what you might ask? The answer is to deal with a potential threat. However, in this case, whatever the threat is, is not clear.

When we experience anxiety and stress during the day, it can trigger old implicit memories. The body does not know how to react because of confusing messages and signals from the body's memory and nervous system. Actions you and the body acted out on in the past didn't bring relief, which means that the body recorded memories of defeat (being unable to regulate itself).

This means the body can freeze in a state of fight or flight or hide. As the body continues to perceive unidentified threats and triggers, it continues to stay on high alert. The body has not regulated these survival responses. Therefore, the body becomes overwhelmed with stress which also can equal anxiety. This is frustrating, as the body cannot calm itself, especially from a past perceived threat, which is not real anymore. The body does not immediately realize all these details.

Maybe you also experienced trauma in the past, which happened during nighttime. So, the body interprets darkness as feeling unsafe and perhaps even with danger. Also, keep in mind we already have a strong predisposition to fear darkness. So, this traumatic memory could also be associated with darkness and danger. If you observe our ancestors hundreds of years ago, you notice that they always slept next to a fire. They never slept in complete darkness because if they did, they could not see any threats and defend themselves. This is also a very strong biological reaction. The more stressed the body is, the more sensitive it is to any programmed biological threats.

You feel responsible for another person's happiness

Something that you can surely relate to is that when a person feels stressed, it's often related to childhood! So, buckle, we are going there now. When you have strong patterns relating to feeling responsible for another person's happiness, then it's possible that caregivers during your childhood made you feel directly or indirectly responsible for their happiness. This could have taken when a caregiver would be upset if you did something. They may have told you to do something and if you didn't, they would then be upset and possibly act in ways that would cause you to feel rejected.

Over time, you might associate taking certain actions as pleasing your caregivers and then getting love, attention, acceptance, or unmet needs met. This becomes a subconscious program. You act and behave in certain ways that are pleasing to other people, even though it conflicts with your needs and your desires. The benefit, or at least a subconscious benefit, is to avoid confrontation, rejection, and to be accepted. Deep down, rejection is one of the biggest fears we have in life. If we don't belong somewhere or cannot identify with a family, community, or someone, it can cause feelings of loss. You can feel meaningless. We have such a strong biological desire to live in groups. In groups, each person has a purpose and value they bring to the community.

This is hard-wired in our DNA. In groups, we also relate and rely on each other for safety. In the ancestry, if they ever excluded you from a group, it could lead to your death. With this newfound isolation, you have to look for shelter, water, and food on your own which drastically decreases your chances of survival. This triggers the fear of dying. This is why people often go to such great lengths to be accepted and not rejected. Deep down on a biological survival level, you are avoiding the fear of dying. It's a purely biological response and not one that makes conscious sense.

However, this fear and experience make perfect sense to the body. We've become so disconnected from the body, looking for ways to cope and deal with pain factors we have in life. We learned to no longer listen to what the body needs and what it's feeling. If we did, this would allow us to take the correct action to resolve challenges that the body is feeling. Instead, we are constantly taking incorrect actions to deal with a problem. You might find short-term solutions to the discomfort that you are feeling, which can give you temporary psychological relief. However, that relief is not enough for the body to overcome the source that caused the unmet need.

Sensitive people who are caring and empathize naturally want others to be happy too. Such kinds of people care for other people's well-being. Caring for other people is a wonderful trait, but it can easily become unhealthy. Taking responsibility for other people's happiness is a big cause of anxiety.

Toxic guilt

Toxic guilt is the best word to describe feeling responsible for other people's happiness. People who are suffering from anxiety experience this type of guilt in which they feel responsible for the happiness of other people around them. Because of excessive thinking, they feel that if other people are going through something bad, then it is because of them. They take responsibility for other people's sorrow, and, therefore, try to take responsibility for their happiness too. Anxiety causes people to become hyperactive in noticing changes in other people's behavior, facial expressions, and voice tone. As anxiety causes people to overthink, they also overthink about the changes in other people's behavior, and even if they notice a slight change, they assume it is their fault. They take responsibility for this.

Anxiety causes people to become very sensitive and makes them prone to experience toxic guilt. Guilt is a feeling people experience when they think that they have done something they should not have done. Or when they think that they have not met other people's expectations. In this case, guilt can be felt when people think they have done something which they should not have done and that they have failed. Feeling responsible for another person's happiness, well-being, and health or feeling guilty for events that are occurring in another person's life, or not being able to meet other people's expectations, standards or judgment is toxic guilt. Toxic guilt also causes people to feel guilty for their feelings.

It also surfaces when people want to please other people. Anxiety makes them prone to think that they're not enough, so they need other people to constantly reassure them they are doing well enough in life. This causes people to have more control over the anxiety-ridden people, and then they can easily manipulate them and make them feel guilty. Toxic guilt makes it difficult for people to say no, and they do not prioritize themselves.

Obsessing over another person's well-being or circumstances can exacerbate or trigger anxiety. It can also make you feel guilty for having things in your life that another person does not have. You may try to obsess over how to change their situation or help them beyond your own limits. It is important to remember that not all victims need to be saved. There are many people in our lives who exploit us and gain our empathy and compassion. Not all people are bad, and they want to hurt us, but if we prioritize people more than ourselves, then we won't even have the capacity to be emotionally supportive.

The dark side of rejection

This is another loop cycle that can become problematic. Earlier, I explained how rejection trauma could often be equivalent to the fear of dying. Because it has a very close relationship with survival?

Rejection trauma can often stem from childhood. A parent dynamic may not have been emotionally fulfilling and emotionally secure. This may have resulted in a time when a child may have needed to feel safe. A rejecting response from a parent has not met their need for safety. This can cause a child to feel rejected instead of feeling comforted and safe. Subconsciously, this can cause a program such as needing to feel safe = rejection. It translates into the body when it needs to feel safe. The conclusion is instead of feeling safe, it floods the body with memories of when rejection was felt.

What happens now? There is a strong possibility that rejection can trigger fear of dying. It activates an ancient inherited response to rejection from the ancestry. So not only can a need for safety = rejection, but it can also become associated with fear of dying.

This might make no sense to the logical mind, and rightfully so. The reason being is that this is subconscious programming that is being referred to. We do not retrieve this type of memory consciously, but subconsciously. That is why you might feel panic when you feel anxiety. This could be one of many reasons people have panic attacks. The body feels there could be a potential for it to die if it feels rejected. This trigger could also activate a deep ancestral survival memory. As you probably already understand, there is a possibility that your need for safety = rejection, abandonment, etc. Then the loop starts. When you feel unsettled and need to feel safe, it triggers implicit memories from the past. Conclusion? The very thing you want, you fear. That can set in panic. The body feels unable to regulate itself and find safety.

You always feel tired when you are around people

Being around people can cause you to feel you are struggling with your energy levels. You may feel extremely drained, even just after having a conversation with someone. This stems from the subconscious mind feeling extremely powerless and not having healthy and clear boundaries. Because of this, there's no real psychological boundary between you and the other person. If you don't have boundaries, you don't have energetic boundaries, period. Do you know that vibe we feel of others when we meet them? You feel it, but you can't explain it?

When you have poor boundaries, in this case (most people who struggle with anxiety have poor boundaries), you will feel vulnerable in the presence of most people. You might feel their vibe without them saying anything. If they are feeling negative, then you might feel their vibe like a weight in your energetic space. Their actions and their words can also drastically affect you.

This symptom also can be true for people who have carried a tremendous amount of responsibility in the past. This can include feeling responsible for people's happiness. In most cases, your association with human connection is negative. It might remind the body of memories of when you felt exhausted, overly responsible, and burdened by other people's problems and challenges, which became your responsibilities and challenges. However, because of your boundary failures, you took on someone else's stress. Over time, it wears you out, and the body remembers this. It is anchored in these negative memories in order for you to avoid similar situations and, in this case, people in the future. The downside is that when you connect with people, the subconscious mind becomes triggered and looks for past associations connecting with people. Then it brings up negative memories where you felt all these burdening responsibility challenges. This can include something as simple as feeling responsible all the time for making someone happy. Responsibility, exhaustion, tiredness, overwhelm, and the body biochemically reacts as if you are back in that same memory again. The drained feeling you felt in the past becomes your boundary. That's your body saying I don't want to be burdened anymore. I don't want to feel responsible for people's happiness anymore. What your body is doing is, it is shouting at you, "we need to work on our boundaries!"

Being around other people in social gatherings is not a simple task, and it requires energy. Social interactions can make a person feel drained and exhausted. You might feel stressed, angry, irritable, or physically tired. It can make you feel you do not have the energy to get out of bed and face people.

Being around people requires a lot of attention, and people who are suffering from anxiety find it difficult to interact with people along with dealing with their thoughts. They have a lot going on in their mind while they are dealing with negative thoughts, and social stress can lead to feeling burdened. Anxiety can cause people to experience emotional exhaustion. Emotional exhaustion can make a person feel emotionally drained and overwhelmed. These feelings can also have physical side effects, such as fatigue. Emotional exhaustion is a feeling which builds up over a long period, and it is very difficult to notice the early warnings of this.

When these feelings pile up and become a colossal mess, then they become clear. It is a common issue that people have little tolerance for other persons' stress or anxiety. This can also leave a stress-ridden person feeling exhausted. Anxiety can cause both physical and emotional effects and it can affect a person's behavior. People become intolerant of others who are suffering from anxiety, so in order to be around such people, an anxiety-ridden person feels they have to pretend they feel balanced when, in fact, they don't. This takes up a lot of energy and leaves the person feeling emotionally exhausted.

Anxiety also drains people's energy and can leave them unable to complete normal life activities. People suffering from anxiety do not have the energy to deal with other people or reciprocate their energy at certain times, so they end up feeling tired around people. This causes them to avoid social gatherings, and they feel more comfortable being alone, so they can process their feelings and do not have to pretend to feel ok.

I have also noticed that when I am suffering from anxiety, interactions with other people drain me. I think that the reason for this is that I feel other people cannot understand my emotions and the state I am going through. The last thing I also want is for people to feel sorry for me. I hate that shit! I know it feels easier to pretend than to explain to them how you feel. But hiding your feelings is very draining as they pile up, and it drains you emotionally and physically. What I have learned throughout this is to never allow someone to feel sorry for you. When they do, it means they can't see your strength and potential to turn your life around. So, screw them. It's ok to be tired, and it's ok to need your own personal space. Make sure that you make allowance for human connection.

Because through the right connections, we can find deep healing experiences.

Your body's instinctive responses are in conflict

Instinctive responses are vital for our survival, and they keep us alive. We can have more than one instinctive response fire off. Example: you run, then seconds later, you feel compelled to hide. In modern research, they refer to fight-and -ht. In my research regarding anxiety and why it can become a long-term pattern, we can experience what is called conflict between instinctive responses.

These conflicted responses can become stuck. Example: when you experience a stressful event, your instinctive response is activated. Something triggered an instinctive response before your emotional response. This happens whether you are conscious of it or not. Something triggers involuntary reactions, and you do not consciously think at that moment if you are going to run or hide; it just happens. If you had to think every time about which instinctive response to act on, you probably would not be alive right now. No conscious thinking is required, no conscious thought or intervention. Your body reacts, it just happens.

When referring to conflicting instinctive responses, it means that more than one instinctive reaction was triggered. When this happens, the body feels overwhelmed, not knowing which instinctive reaction to act out on in order to help you move into a safer place. Instead, the body can get become stuck in a state of distress. It panics because it doesn't know which reaction to process first, and even two or three responses can be triggered and be in conflict. Until these instinctive responses are resolved, the body can stay in a state of stress and anxiety. In this example, it does not mean that a person is stuck in a full-blown state of fight, flight, or hide. It means that the body feels conflicted about which response to revert to, to regulate itself after a stressful event, or the onset of an anxious episode.

Chapter 6

Anxiety and fatigue

The effects of anxiety are not limited to psychological problems, as anxiety can easily manifest as physical symptoms such as muscle tension, difficulty sleeping, or a fast heartbeat. Anxiety can also result in fatigue. The mind and body are not two separate things. They are tied in. The mind has a huge effect on the body and vice versa. They're connected in significant ways. Anxiety can manifest as various physical symptoms, such as headaches, feeling weak, sweating, trembling, or shaking, hyperventilation, muscle tension, and digestive problems. Chronic anxiety is a common cause of fatigue as it has different effects on the body which are adverse. There are a lot of reasons why anxiety causes fatigue. Adrenaline kicks in when a person experiences stress and anxiety, and the sympathetic nervous system kicks in and causes the heart to race and the breathing rate increases. This also results in an increase in stress hormones, such as adrenaline.

Adrenaline handles the body's fight-or-flight response. It makes you feel energized during an episode of anxiety, but when it wears off, it makes you feel more tired than usual. This is referred to as an "adrenaline crash". When a person is suffering from anxiety, they feel their thoughts are racing, and they are always on high alert. This takes a lot of mental energy, and avoiding it even takes more energy. When a lot of energy is invested into these feelings and into controlling them, it results in a mental fog, and people have difficulty concentrating on different tasks. This is referred to as "mental exhaustion," and it can make a person physically tired. Anxiety can also cause muscle tension. This happens because of the fight-or-flight response, which is triggered by the body so that it is ready to respond to a harmful situation. As the body stays in a constant mode of tension, it causes muscle tension, which results in physical fatigue.

You are overly conscious of what others think of you and your opinions

This is especially true if your self-esteem and your ability to decide in the past have been criticized and put down. If so, you will have a heightened sensitivity in the future to people criticizing or judging you. Why does this pack a hard emotional punch? Your opinion, beliefs, and values are all expressions of the depth of who you are. It is showing others what you think and feel. When we show this side of ourselves, we can feel vulnerable because we are exposing our true nature and authentic self. Your opinions can be judged or even attacked. People can criticize beliefs and values.

You can take this personally because it feels like an attack on your identity, worth, who you are, and what you stand for. It begs the question, "could there be a prior experience that caused you to feel this way? Did something happen that made you feel that what you had to share was not good enough?" The result? You might feel you always have to fight for your truth, which is exhausting. Everyone's feedback might feel like an attack, which can cause you to feel you always have to be on defense and ready for fight-or-flight. It's a pattern that can drain anyone's soul.

Anxiety and social approval

Human beings are also called social animals because we are social species. On average, four out of five processes going on in the background of our brain are about relationships with other people we care about a lot because it affects our relationships and being humans' relationships are very important for emotional well-being. Being social, humans worry about what others think. We want to be in everyone's good books so we can nurture relationships with them. The reason we worry about what other people think of us is that we have a fear that people might leave us. As I mentioned earlier in this book, the fear of rejection can be felt similar to the fear of dying.

Anxiety makes people overly conscious of what others think of them and their opinions. Although, it should not matter what other people think of us as they do not know what struggles we are going through, and they are unaware of our problems as well. We are the only person who knows all our problems and difficulties. Therefore, we should only care about what we think of ourselves instead of what others think. Many of us feel anxious because we are worried about what other people will think of us. For example, if you are extremely anxious before speaking publicly, walking through a room of strangers, or raising your hand in a meeting is because you are worried about social disapproval.

When we fear other people's opinions a lot, it becomes an irrational and unproductive session. It is in human nature to crave societal approval. It is something that has been passed down to us by our ancestors. Even thousands of years ago, if the responsibility for a failed hunt fell on your shoulders, your place in the tribe could be threatened. You might be judged as weak or not good enough, which triggers rejection. Humans have developed a desire to fit in, and it has caused a fear of being disliked by other people. We undermine our abilities and pursue to make other people happy and win their remarks. This causes a lot of anxiety, as we are continuously worried about what other people will think of us.

At some level, it is good to think about what other people think of us because studies show that people are more likely to be kind and considerate if they have experienced embarrassment and shame. However, chronically worrying too much about what other people think of us is not a good habit. Studies show that people constantly overestimate themselves. It deprives people of joy in life. It is a common saying that " hurt people hurt people." On a personal level, I believe that this statement is very accurate. Sometimes, even if we do everything in our power to make others happy, we fail.

Sometimes people are happy being unhappy. It is possible that what others think of us is not a reflection of our doings, but rather a reflection of themselves and their inner state. Sometimes people only behave in ways they know how to if they could behave better than they would have. Even if you do your best to be kind and considerate, it is possible to be judged negatively by others. Knowing this, we can be a little more compassionate towards others and very little about what they think of us.

You don't feel safe to relax

You feel it is not safe to relax, and you feel tension throughout your body. This is also a very strong pattern when we observe symptoms of anxiety. It might be a pattern that you can relate to. Sometimes, you feel you have to be doing something. Something should happen right now. There is this unresolved sense of urgency that you could never shake off. Almost like something was very important, and you missed an important task or deadline. This could be because you do not have a positive association with calmness. Have you ever thought about that? You might not have a positive association with feeling relaxed. Why?

Because maybe in the past, when you did, something bad may have happened.

When you were happy or relaxed, a caregiver might always have been up your ass, such as fighting with you or saying something to disrupt your peace. They may have always done or said something to insult or humiliate you. Caregivers might have had a toxic style of using fear to motivate and encourage you in life. There may have been moments when you would sit down and watch TV or do something that was calming for you.

A caregiver might provoke you or start an argument, causing you to leave the house. Maybe you never realized it, but your body never felt safe to be calm and relaxed. Why? When you are calm, your defense mechanisms are not as fast and sharp to act as when they are when you are stressed and on high alert. It was easier to stay in a state of distress because then you could not be surprised. I was always ready to fight and defend myself. I felt safer being stressed and alert than feeling calm. Can you relate to this?

You feel people can easily manipulate you and you feel powerless to change it

This is especially true because in the past, when you perhaps expressed boundaries, it was not well received. When you expressed yourself or an opinion, there could've been a very dominant figure around you that completely put you down or punished you. So, what happens? We associate our need to take action with memories associated with feeling like a failure. Continuing to take action triggers these memories of failure. That is why you sometimes feel that you had failed before you even started. This would be a disempowering experience for most people. It's a cycle of frustration and feeling held back by strong unresolved experiences.

Unfortunately, we live in a society where it is very difficult to relax. The demands of our everyday life are never-ending. Society has trained us to run after success, achievement, and goals. We take out very little time to relax daily. This puts our body and mind under constant pressure. When we run after materialistic gains in life, we forget it is important to relax. Even if we analyze our day, it is evident that we take little to no time for ourselves. By doing this, we train our minds to constantly be in work mode. If the mind gets no rest and time to cool down, then all our emotions and feelings bubble up, and when the brain cannot take it any longer, all our emotions become difficult to control. It becomes difficult to relax, and anxiety spreads throughout the body.

Why it's so hard to relax

Anxiety is a feeling characterized by the production of hormones in the body that induce stress. Anxiety causes the parasympathetic nervous system to release hormones that activate the flight-or-fight response. When our brain stays in defense mode, it becomes difficult to relax as our nervous systems are high on stress hormones. The rush of these hormones makes the nervous system feel that it is not OK, and it is not safe to relax.

The brain perceives this as a threatening situation, so it does not calm down and stays in a constant fight-or-flight response. Anxiety is associated with feelings of constant fear and stress. This interferes with the body's natural relaxation mechanisms, making it difficult to relax and calm down. Anxiety is also characterized by overthinking. It causes the brain to become foggy.

The brain is constantly flooded with disturbing information, which induces stress. If you are not treating your anxiety, then living with untreated anxiety makes things more challenging. Constant stress and worry make it difficult for a person to relax. Symptoms of anxiety that make it difficult to relax are difficulty focusing or concentrating on things, procrastinating because you feel overwhelmed, and avoiding different situations because they make you feel anxious and overwhelmed and unable to relax.

This makes it difficult for a person to be by themselves and enjoy some downtime. The symptoms of anxiety contribute to an inability to relax. When these symptoms combine and overlap, it leaves a person feeling helpless, and then a feeling of restlessness and overthinking creates a state of stress which hinders the body's natural relaxation response.

People who suffer from anxiety experience more stress from the thought of relaxing. Stress relaxation is a new word that has been used for when a person feels overwhelmed when they try to relax. Stress relaxation describes relaxation-induced anxiety. It is shown to happen to between 30% to 50% of people. It is a paradox that when people who experience relaxation-induced anxiety, they try to relax.

Instead of relaxing, it makes them feel more anxious, which turns into a destructive cycle where they cannot do anything to relieve their stress. Not everyone who experiences anxiety is prone to stress relaxation, but some researchers suggest that anxiety and stress relaxation are closely intertwined.

Some other reasons apart from anxiety which can cause a feeling similar to stress-induced anxiety can be that people are worried about what other people will say if they take out time to relax or they can simply not decide about what to do to relax.

Chapter 7

Probable causes of anxiety-The body's response

We will explore anxiety that could stem from inherited anxiety and unresolved trauma from your past. Unidentified fear (meaning memories from your subconscious mind that are triggered) is the number one cause, especially if the fear is stuck in your subconscious mind. It stems from an implicit memory (implicit memory means that a deep subconscious memory has been triggered, and the body biochemically reacts to it). You feel the fear of this old memory. You can feel discomfort in your body, and this sensation can result from an old memory being activated.

This memory can sometimes be the worst of memories to have activated. You feel distress, and you look at your environment, but there's nothing in your environment to validate why you feel how you do. Then we wonder and think, is it our intuition trying to warn us? Did we just miss a sign of danger? Am I in the right place at the right time? All these thoughts can run through your mind. The doubt that you might have felt toward the uncertainty of not understanding what the body is trying to say magnifies the anxiety that you are feeling. In moments like this, it is helpful to immediately observe your environment when you feel anxious. Ask yourself, "Do I see something that validates how I am feeling right now?

Do I see evidence why I should feel how I do?" This simple exercise can bring a significant change. It can help you work through waves of anxiety that you would have felt at that moment instead of feeling powerless towards the anxiety. What also makes the waves of anxiety even more frustrating is that they can cause you to feel more fearful and mistrusting.

The body's pessimistic wiring

It's the body's natural program to be negative and to be pessimistic. That includes often expecting the worst. How strongly this is felt will vary from person to person depending on whether their parents were examples of this. So, when you have this underlying program running in the background as well as activated negative memories, it can exasperate your current state of anxiety.

What happens next? You feel overwhelmed. So, we look for escape mechanisms and ways to cope with how we feel. We look for easy ways to find comfort. We don't always understand the underlying problem of why we feel anxious.

Sometimes you feel you are in a room, and you are blindfolded, twirled around ten times, and then you are told to find the exit. The result? You can only imagine, I bet. When you are confused, then finding solutions in that state is counterproductive. You will end up applying the wrong methods to deal with anxiety. Therefore, we continue to misfire, finding the correct solution to create a lasting positive outcome.

We often wonder why people are so pessimistic. The reason for this is that humans are pessimistic by default. Science has proven that we, by nature, are pessimistic. This means that if we do not know how to deal with the complexity of our mind and care for our mental health, we go back to our pessimistic default state.

Even when most of us evaluate our day, we focus more on what went wrong rather than what went right. In reality, we have more things going right than wrong in our daily life. This is something that we do not develop but are born with.

Even if children are asked a few questions, and they get some wrong, they focus more on the ones they got wrong. We focus more on our drawbacks, and we grow up with this trend as well. When we feel stuck in life, we focus on darkness more than we focus on light. Pessimism is universal, and it is ancestral. It dates to the Ice Age.

Humans dealt with life-threatening situations like extreme cold, ice, famine, and floods. The pessimism and stress from what our species went through seem to have been shaved down to other generations as well.

The pessimism which humans develop to avoid distress is known as defensive pessimism. It is a coping technique that is used by individuals who set low expectations for situations. Negative pessimism elevates an individual's anxiety about situations. They create self-fulfilling prophecies, and their negative pessimism motivates them to plan ways to avoid chances of poor outcomes. It prepares a human to expect and plan for the worst-case scenario to avoid it. People who have defensive pessimism have low expectations and they thoroughly explore potential failures because of their anxiety.

Defensive pessimism differs from normal pessimism. Defensive pessimists have negative beliefs that bad things happen because of them. They fixate on their shortcomings, have low self-esteem, and have difficulty taking risks or finding motivation. Pessimism creates an increased risk of anxiety.

Pessimists are inflexible to their feelings and thinking, but defensive pessimists can reflect on their situations and plan for anything. Defensive pessimism means assuming a bad outcome and preparing yourself accordingly. It helps as a coping technique because it enables you to prepare for the worst beforehand. If it is used knowingly, then it can work better as a coping technique. Otherwise, you won't have control over it, and it will make you feel pessimistic all the time.

Pessimism can also be referred to as something humans develop to survive. It allows us to prepare for the worst. It helps us to be adaptive to survival. Therefore, it is something that has been hard-wired in our minds. Unless we consciously develop emotional intelligence skills, our brains become automatically programmed like our ancestors. We sense, act, think, and feel the same way. We focus more on the negativity of the world instead of focusing our energy on the positive aspects of life.

Unresolved fear and threat detection

Fear is a natural response to trauma because the body seeks to protect itself from perceived threats. In this moment of trauma, if you had no support, a compassionate witness, or access to inner emotional resources that would allow you to feel safe and supported to overcome a traumatic event, that is when the event becomes a traumatic stored memory. However, if you had support or could act wisely to overcome the event, to feel safe again. What does that mean? It means you are moving toward becoming resilient in relation to the traumatic experience you had. What this means is if you ever had to find yourself in a similar situation again, you would feel much stronger and more confident about dealing with it.

There is a slight twist. This also depends on your ancestral predispositions, coping mechanisms, and your state of mind on the day when you experienced the traumatic event. It depends on what kind of trauma you experienced as well. Did it have a direct potential impact on a life-or-death situation, or whether it was an emotional threat? I dive deep into this during my MAT 1 Technique. When you experience trauma, the body reacts in fear because, in most cases, it's uncertain what action to take to resolve the problem, especially if you have no prior experience with this traumatic event. At that moment, the body panics because it is the body's only job to keep you alive. If the body feels like it's failing that one job that it has, it can create tremendous stress, such as anxiety.

The body, especially the nervous system, can overcompensate because of these unresolved traumatic experiences. Let's say, for example, your mother punished you. She smacked you because you wouldn't listen to her. The punishment felt traumatic for you. At the time of this event, there was also a spider in the room, and you saw it. This could mean that you associated the trauma you felt at the time with the spider, even though the spider is completely innocent in this case. It was just in the wrong place at the wrong time. This is a great example of where an unexplained fear of spiders can stem from. The body associated the spider with how upset you felt on the day your mother punished you. There is a strong possibility that you might overact when you see a spider again.

Your stress response to anxiety

This is a brilliant question and a very important one to answer. I spent so much time trying to understand and resolve the pain points I had. However, I always felt a powerful pull to at least change how I feel about my anxiety rather than the anxiety itself. I broke up my healing journey into steps. I realized that our thoughts and how our stress response system responds to them lock us in our negative perspective of life.

Let's start with the stress response in the body, as this is a big culprit behind our negative thoughts. A stress response often starts through our sensory skills, which include the brain. When you experience heightened levels of stress, your senses will send information to the amygdala, which is our panic button. The amygdala also helps us process emotional data and information from our environment. The amygdala then interprets sounds and images that it receives from your sensory system.

When it detects danger, sends hormonal stress signals to the hypothalamus. The hypothalamus is basically what experts would call the command center. This part of the brain will then communicate with the rest of the body through the nervous system. It will release cortisol and adrenaline to take action if necessary.

This part of the brain will show your lungs to inhale more air. Your blood pressure could change, and your heartbeat could increase. The autonomic nervous system, which is then also tapped on and activated, splits into two branches. One is called the sympathetic nervous system, and the other branch is called the parasympathetic nervous system. The sympathetic nervous system is like a wild stallion. It's always ready to go! It sets off our flight-and-fight response, giving the body the gasoline that it needs to take action.

The parasympathetic nervous system is like someone on a long-extended holiday on the beach. This nervous system likes to chill and relax, and it also soothes the body after a stressful event, like a glass of wine. We have a hormone called epinephrine released into the blood, and it causes physiological changes in your heart, blood pressure, muscles, and vital organs. The small airways in your lungs also open wide, hence why suddenly you take deep breaths. This allows extra oxygen to be sent to the brain, allowing you to be guarded and aware of your environment. It also sharpens all your other senses.

On the flip side, the sympathetic nervous system, which is also called the wild stallion, needs to be reined in, controlled and calmed down. Normally, the stress response takes at least 20 minutes to calm down and reset itself before the body can slowly regulate itself. In most cases, what happens when we feel stress can escalate, especially when it has triggered prior old memories related to unresolved trauma or stress.

When they are activated, these old memories can release a biochemical response throughout the body, releasing memories concerning how you responded to that stress in the past. Your body is biochemically relieving that stress to a certain degree again.

Often, in most cases, these subconscious unresolved stress-related memories are implicit. What does that mean? It means that you do not have a conscious cognitive recollection of why you feel how you do. All that you know is that you feel bad, stressed, or anxious. These old memories can now exasperate your current anxiety and stress that you're feeling.

However, in most cases, it is old unresolved trauma and stress from the past. It is experienced as anxiety in your present life because your environment is triggering these trigger buttons in your subconscious mind. Why certain specific memories? Because your mind focuses on what you energize. If you worry, then your mind will continue to tap into fearful memories, hence why they are more likely to be triggered rather than a positive memory. Many people do not realize when they experience anxiety that they are (in most cases, not all) reliving the past and projecting old, unresolved stress and fears from the past into their present moment. Then, we make decisions in this stressed state that influences our future. This is how we keep the past alive.

Let's talk about why and how your negative thoughts cause your life and world to look so bleak. Research has shown that when you feel stressed, the Reticular Activating System, known as the RAS, filters information from your environment based on what you're focusing on. So, what does that mean? If you are anxious and you feel depressed, then your RAS will align with people, images, and circumstances that will validate how you feel. This only reinforces negative thoughts that you already have. Once these negative emotions and thoughts are reinforced, it continues to lock in the RAS to stay focused on information from your environment that will reflect how you feel.

You must have noticed that when you are furious, it's really hard to see how beautiful the day might be and hear children laugh. Instead, you see the opposite. This is how our stress response, and the RAS can play a very important role in this case. To change and influence this process positively, it requires conscious mindfulness practices to change your thoughts. To refocus on something that is more positive, however, we will jump a little later into that aspect.

The body's primary motive is to feel safe

We all want to be and feel safe. That is normal and something that we all are emotionally and biologically programmed for. However, think now for a minute. What if your experience and your association with needing to feel safe were negative? When you wanted to feel safe, people reacted to you in a way that made you feel more upset, rejected, abandoned, or even unsafe. You form a negative association with the very thing that you need, which is safety. For the next day or two, when you need to feel safe, think about what you expect in return. Do you expect to feel safe? In most cases, the answer is no. When a person needs to feel safe, more negative emotions arise from that need. If that is the case, then your response is revealing to you what your associations are with feeling safe.

Something has negatively met your need for safety. What does this mean? Look at the loop which is now being created. This loop can cause anxiety, and it can cause anxiety to become stuck. When you need safety and your need for safety is met by trauma, and you cannot overcome that traumatic event, the body locks in this anxiety and feeling unsafe. In the future, when you are in a similar situation again, and you want to feel safe, whether it's conscious or subconscious, your mind will search the subconscious mind for prior memories associated with needing safety so you can relate to it.

What do you think is going to happen? Triggers of memories of feeling unsafe trigger the memories of the trauma associated with the time that you needed to feel safe. Which then triggers the feeling of being unsafe again. Your need for safety is not being met. The body feels anxious because it cannot find balance and safety. This is a very important observation. In short, needing to feel safe = negative experiences meet your need for safety.

Chapter 8

Anxiety's effect on health

Stress and anxiety can have a tremendous impact on our health, and then ultimately, our quality of life. When your body is always in a state of fight-and-flight, it means that there's continued cortisol and adrenaline being released, and you reach a heightened state of awareness. If we do not learn how to release accumulated stress to regulate the body and become calm again, the body then uses more energy and resources. This means that if we have a poor diet, the body pulls resources and minerals from its reserves. The body depletes itself because the sources from which your body is pulling energy are not being replenished fast enough. We also have a threshold in relation to how much stress we can handle. That threshold will push back at some point and let you know you are living a life beyond your psychological and energetic capacity.

Musculoskeletal system

Stress has been shown to affect the musculoskeletal system, respiratory, cardiovascular, endocrine, gastrointestinal, nervous system, and reproductive systems. These are well-known facts. That is why we have dived so deeply into learning and understanding how psychosomatic stress can exasperate ailments and illnesses in the physical body.

Our muscles help us move, walk, talk, and blink our eyes. We have voluntary and involuntary muscles. We even have muscles that are connected to our instinctive responses to help us act and react during moments of threat. Our muscles can even react to our emotions.

Have you noticed when you become furious or upset, your muscles feel tense? You might feel shoulder pain, back pain, or even a headache. The reason is that the muscle has a reflex and responds to the stress that you are feeling. Normally, you will feel this type of reflex when you have an accident, or you are about to fall. However, it's learned through research that when you feel emotionally rigid or are resistant to something in your life, the body and the muscles react with the rigid tension. So, when you have neck pain or back pain, ask yourself when did it start and what were you resisting in your life? Something to think about.

If you observe tension headaches and migraines, they are associated with chronic muscle tension. This tension often originates from your shoulders, neck, and head area. It can even be from the lower back. Please keep in mind that this is not necessarily always the case for migraines! Migraines can be diet related and because of so many other causes. This is just one of many examples that research has noticed in people who struggle with fear-based anxiety. This fear-based response results in a person having an oversensitivity to general physical pain. Why? Well, this is a brilliant question.

It has been observed that it often relates to a person who already has a sensitivity to emotional pain and stress. The fear of bad things happening, such as a fear of being in an accident, fear of reliving the past, and fear of feeling further discomfort. That is because this person's threshold and ability to cope and deal with stress and pain-related stress have reached their capacity. Therefore, there can be an oversensitivity to pain. There are patterns where people would feel perhaps a prick of a needle and not necessarily be bothered by it, versus someone who suffers from anxiety would have a much more emotional reaction to it.

It is a common phenomenon that when the body is stressed, then the muscles tense. Muscle tension is a reflex reaction to stress. It is the body's way of protecting itself from injury and pain. If you experience sudden stress, muscles tense up all at once and release their tension when the stress passes.

Chronic stress causes the muscles of the body to remain tensed all the time. The body remains in a constant state of guardedness. When the muscles stay tense for a longer period, it triggers a lot of negative reactions in the body and promotes a lot of stress-related disorders. Both tension-type headaches and migraine headaches are also associated with chronic muscle tension in the areas of the neck, head, and shoulders. It has also linked musculoskeletal pain in the lower back to stress.

Respiratory system

Our lungs are deeply connected to our fight-or-flight response. When we experience stress, the small air sacs in the lungs become bigger, allowing more air and oxygen to flow into the lungs and the brain. It allows our senses to become sharpened. We are moving into a new state of alertness. If you suffer from anxiety right now, you are probably breathing shallowly. It is guaranteed that you're not using your lungs to their fullest capacity. Please take a deep breath right now. Did your lungs feel tight when you did that? Did you feel you got enough air? If you can take a deep breath easily, then it means you are relatively relaxed. If you were not able to, you might ask why that is the case.

When we suffer from anxiety, it means that the body is always ready for fight-and-flight. If your lungs feel restricted right now, it means that you are most likely stuck in the hide response, also known as an instinctive response. It could show signs of vulnerability and not feeling 100% settled within yourself. That is because, subconsciously, your mind and body are on full alert. It feels like you are waiting for the other shoe to drop.

Your mind is confused because it can see no threat in its environment to validate why you feel how you do. This only exasperates the anxiety that you're feeling because the body feels like it should prepare itself for a threat that is not there. Have you ever seen an animal that is stressed and it's hiding? You can Google it on YouTube, and you'll notice and see that their breathing is quick and very shallow. That is because they are in the hide response. They don't feel safe.

Our lungs react the same way. People who stress a lot and suffer from anxiety might have lung challenges such as bronchitis, obstructive pulmonary disease, emphysema, chronic bronchitis, and asthma. If you have ever had a panic attack and you hyperventilated, this shows another example of how emotions can try to be expressed through the body. A reaction like that would mean there's a part of you that's tired of hiding, and you're ready to change. However, you are stuck in fear. There are people with hyperventilating challenges who have panic attacks in moments of their lives when they want to create change. However, they fear the next step.

Studies have even shown how extreme stress, such as the passing of a pet or loved one, can trigger an asthma attack in someone who has never had asthma before.

Cardiovascular system

The cardiovascular system comprises two components which are the heart and the blood vessels. The heart and the blood vessels collaboratively work together to provide nourishment and oxygen to the organs of the body. The activity of the heart and blood vessels is also coordinating the body's response to stress. Short-term stress, which lies on the lower spectrum of anxiety, causes an increase in heart rate and stronger contractions of the heart muscles, which releases stress hormones such as adrenaline, cortisol, and noradrenaline.

For example, if we experience short-term stress, such as meeting deadlines, being stuck in traffic, falling from a stair, or slamming on the brakes to avoid an accident, we experience that our heart rate increases, and we feel stressed.

When the body experiences stress, the blood vessels that direct blood to muscles and the heart dilate. It increases the amount of blood pumped to these parts of the body, and that increases blood pressure. When the fight-or-flight response of the body is activated, the heart rate also increases and when this episode has passed.

The body returns to its normal state. However, chronic stress, which is experienced over a long period, can contribute to long-term problems for the heart and blood vessels. With chronic stress, the body remains in a fight-or-flight response almost all the time. This increases blood pressure and negatively affects the health of the cardiovascular system. Long-term stress also increases the risk of hypertension, heart attack, or stroke, the elevated levels of blood pressure, which is caused because of the elevated level of stress hormones.

Persistent chronic stress and continuous acute stress can also contribute to inflammation in the cardiovascular system. It can lead to inflammation in the circulatory system, particularly in the coronary arteries. When the body experiences stress, cholesterol levels are also elevated. It increases the risk of heart disease. In women, the effect of stress on the cardiovascular system differs or three menopausal or post-menopausal women. For pre-menopausal women, the body has an elevated level of estrogen.

This helps the blood vessels to respond better during stress. So, it prepares the body to handle stress better and protects it against heart disease. But for post-menopausal women, the body does not have an elevated level of estrogen, and it loses its protection, and such women are at greater risk of the effects of stress on heart disease.

Stress can affect the heart. There are people who almost drew themselves to a heart attack because of their grief and other emotions. Emotions, trauma, stress, grief, and their impact on the body are tremendous. The heart works in a compromised way with two sections of the cardiovascular system that work together as a team. It brings nutrition and oxygen to the organs of the body. Strong negative emotions such as anxiety and anger can cause your heart rate to increase and the heart muscle to contract, challenging the muscle.

Keep in mind that your heart is a muscle, and when you work a muscle too much or too little, and then suddenly you work it very hard again, it sends inconsistent messages to the memory of the heart tissue. This can set anyone up for potential heart problems. Women suffer more from heart problems than men.

Observation shows that this is because men are biologically strongly wired to cope and deal with high levels of stress. When you look at our ancestors, men were the ones who fought, defended, worked, and protected. Women were caretakers and the support system in the family. Men also have more testosterone, allowing them to endure harsher circumstances. If women had to move into that same masculine state, it would pressure the body, especially the heart, gut, and immune system response.

Endocrine system

When you find yourself in circumstances that require you to take action to stay safe, your brain is going to send correct hormonal stress responses to the rest of the body in order to act and react. Here, the endocrine system can be deeply affected because it involves the hypothalamus. It also involves the pituitary and the adrenal, known as the HPA axis. These are the primary drivers of the endocrine stress response. When these parts of our stress response system are overworked, it can cause an increased production of steroid hormones called glucocorticoids, which also includes cortisol.

During a stress response, the endocrine system will signal to the adrenal glands above our kidneys to release more cortisol. Cortisol gives us the ability to act and react. It gives us the motivation to take action. Here, glucocorticoids also regulate our immune system, which allows any inflammatory responses that we have in the body to be soothed.

Surely you can put one and one together by now. If you are chronically stressed, it means that your immune system can be challenged and unable to control inflammatory responses in your body. Hence, you might be more susceptible to pain, headaches, and gut problems.

Chronic stress can cause dysfunction in communication between the immune system and the HPA access. This can cause chronic fatigue, metabolic disorders, diabetes, obesity, depression, and immune disorders. By now, you can see the power of our emotions and how anxiety can deeply influence the cellular health of the body.

The HPA Axis

The HPA axis, or hypothalamic-pituitary-adrenal axis is the primary driver of the endocrine stress response. In order to understand how emotional health affects the endocrine system, it is important to evaluate the hypothalamic-pituitary-adrenal axis. When the HPA axis activates the endocrine stress response, it results in an increase in the production of steroid hormones called glucocorticoids, which include cortisol, often referred to as the stress hormone.

During times of prolonged stress, the hypothalamus, endocrine system, and a collection of nuclei that connects the brain to the endocrine system signal the pituitary gland to produce a hormone. This hormone then signals the adrenal glands to increase the production of cortisol. The renal glands are present just above the kidneys.

When cortisol level increases, it influences an increase in the level of energy fuel that is available by mobilizing glucose and fatty acids from the liver. Cortisol provides a cycle of energy throughout the day. The production typically increases in concentration in the morning and slowly declines throughout the day. But during a stressful event, an increase in cortisol can provide the energy required for challenges with a prolonged or extreme challenge.

Chronic stress impairs communication between the immune system and the HPA axis. It has linked the impaired communication to the future development of many physical and mental health conditions which include chronic fatigue, and metabolic disorders like diabetes, obesity, etc.

Gastrointestinal system

If you feel challenged with anxiety, then you might have experienced gut health problems. It could be a chronic challenge or flare-up when you feel strong triggers of anxiety. Sometimes the gut flares up when you feel anxious. How we respond to stress is different for everyone. Research has shown that stress can be associated with changes in gut flora. This can influence your quality of life in relation to your happiness, as 80% of serotonin is produced in the gut and only 20% in the brain.

Serotonin is only one hormonal chemical response that helps us to feel happy. There are other chemicals coming into play. However, the reason this is being mentioned is to share the power of your gut. Therefore, they say if your gut is happy, then you are happy. If you have a good diet, your chances of feeling happier in life also increase.

All of us have experienced that when we feel nervous, it gives us butterflies in our stomachs. Those butterflies show that our brain and the digestive system are related. So, if the mind is experiencing stress, it is evident that our stomach is affected, too. They also referred to the gut as the second brain because it has a nervous system with more neurotransmitters. The brain has a direct impact on the stomach and the intestines.

This can be proven because digestive juices are released in our stomach before the food gets there. It happens when we think about eating. This also makes it easier to understand why we might feel nauseated before giving a presentation. Some people also feel intestinal pain during situations that are stress-inducing. Stress, depression, or other psychological symptoms can affect the movement and contractions of the gastrointestinal tract.

We have discussed several times that anxiety activates the brain's sympathetic nervous system. The sympathetic nervous system activates our fight-or-flight response, which prepares the body to protect itself in an endangering situation. When the fight-or-flight response is activated, the body is on guard. In order to do so, it conserves functions that are not immediately needed for survival. So, it puts digestion on hold. This can lead to stomachache, indigestion, nausea, and heartburn. The stomach slows down, and stress causes the motor function in our large intestine to increase. So, you might experience diarrhea or a bowel emergency.

This can cause a loop, as experiencing these digestive systems can make a person even more stressed, and stress is a cause for these digestive system symptoms. Chronic stress can cause gastrointestinal issues. Although stress does not always cause underlying diseases, it can intensify their symptoms.

In order to overcome our sympathetic nervous system, we need to activate the parasympathetic nervous system. The parasympathetic nervous system does the opposite of the sympathetic nervous system. It makes the body calm, and it makes the heart rate go down. It then also makes the gastrointestinal system function normally.

The connection between the brain and the gastrointestinal system is in two ways. Just as a troubled brain can cause gastrointestinal issues, the same way a troubled stomach can cause brain issues, a person's stomach or intestinal distress can also be a product of anxiety, stress, or depression. If a person is experiencing gastrointestinal issues with no apparent reason, and there are no physical causes to it, then it is very much possible that it is because of anxiety.

How stress affects the esophagus

It is common that when people are stressed, they can eat much more or much less than usual. Stress affects the food intake of people by affecting their gastrointestinal systems. This can cause heartburn or acid reflux. It is also known that intense stress can set off a rare case of spasms in the esophagus, which is so intense that it can easily be mistaken for a heart attack. It also is known that stress can make swallowing foods more difficult or increase the amount of air that is swallowed. This increases burping, gassiness, and bloating.

How stress affects the stomach

Research has proven that stress can make pain, nausea, bloating and other stomach discomforts felt more easily. If stress is severe enough, it can also result in vomiting. Stress also causes a drastic increase or decrease in appetite. This results in unhealthy diet habits and deteriorates one's stomach health.

How stress affects the bowel

Stress can also cause pain, discomfort, or bloating in the bowels. Stress can also affect the speed with which food moves through the body. This can cause either diarrhea or constipation. Stress can also induce muscle spasms in the bowel, which can be extremely painful. Research has proven that stress also affects digestion and which nutrients the intestines absorb. It can also increase gas production related to nutrient absorption in the bowels. The intestines have a defense system to protect the body from food-related bacteria. As we know that stress affects the immune system of the body, it can also make the intestinal barrier weaker, which can allow a lot of bacteria to enter the body. People who are suffering from chronic bowel disorders have severe effects of stress on their symptoms. Stress makes the gut nerves more sensitive, and it changes the gut immune response.

Reproductive system

Stress also affects the reproductive systems of the male body. Chronic stress and deactivation of the fight-or-flight response also affect the reproductive system in the male. This happens because in the male body, when the fight-or-flight response is activated, it produces testosterone and activates the sympathetic nervous system. Testosterone is also responsible for creating arousal in males. Stress can also cause the body to release another hormone, cortisol, which is produced by the adrenal glands. The function of cortisol is to regulate blood pressure to stop the excess amounts of cortisol that affect the normal biochemical functioning of the male reproductive system. Chronic stress also affects testosterone production, resulting in a decline in sex drive, which can cause erectile dysfunction. Chronic stress can also negatively affect sperm production and maturation. It can cause difficulties for a couple to conceive. Researchers have found that men who experienced over two stressful life events in the past year had lost sperm count more than men who did not experience any stressful events. If stress affects the immune system, then the body can become vulnerable to infection. In the male anatomy, infections can also affect reproductive functioning.

Effects of stress on menstruation:

Stress also affects menstruation in women in several ways. High levels of stress are also associated with the absence of or irregularity of menstrual cycles. Stress can also cause more painful periods, and it can also affect the length of cycles. Chronic anxiety may also reduce sexual desire among women. This is more common for women who are caring for young children or other family members and coping with chronic anxiety. Stress also makes premenstrual symptoms worse for women, and as menopause approaches, the levels of hormone in the body fluctuate rapidly. These changes are associated with anxiety, feeling distress, and mood swings. Thus, menopause can also cause more anxiety, and anxiety can worsen the physical symptoms of menopause.

Research has proven that women who are more anxious experience an increased number of hot flashes than women who are not. Stress can also cause several reproductive diseases in women as it affects the immune system. When the immune system is compromised, it is easier to develop diseases of the reproductive system.

Stress can also negatively affect pregnancy. It can cause serious health problems like high blood pressure, which can lead to problems in pregnancy like premature birth. Although it is very common to feel stressed during pregnancy because a pregnant woman's life is experiencing many major changes. Her body and her emotions are changing, and this change can be very overwhelming. High levels of stress, if continued for a long period, can cause health problems like blood pressure and heart problems. If a pregnant woman experiences a lot of stress, then it can cause problems like "premature birth," which is the birth of her child before 37 weeks of pregnancy.

Stress can also lead to a "low birth weight baby," a condition in which a baby weighs less than five pounds and eight ounces. Children who are born "prematurely" or with "low birth weight" are at an increased rate of severe health problems. It does not mean that regular stress during pregnancy, such as daily life problems, will add to pregnancy problems. But serious types of stress can increase health problems.

Anxiety makes it difficult for a pregnant woman to take care of herself and her baby. It is very important for a pregnant woman to care for herself and the well-being of her baby and herself. Besides this, a lot of stress-related hormones play a crucial role in causing several pregnancy complications.

Stress, which is serious and long-lasting, can also affect the immune system. The immune system protects the human body from infections. A damaged immune system can increase the chance of getting infections in the uterus. Such infections can also cause many complications.

Women who are suffering from "post-traumatic stress disorder" are more likely to have a premature or low birth weight baby than a woman without it. Women who suffer from post-traumatic stress disorder also have risky health behaviors, such as abusing medications, taking drugs, smoking cigarettes, or consuming alcohol. These behaviors can also cause many complications with childbirth.

Research has also shown that if a mother experiences a lot of stress during pregnancy, it can cause problems during childhood. Such children may have difficulty paying attention in school, for example. If a pregnant woman experiences stress, it can also affect the brain development end the immune system development of the baby.

Chronic stress can also have negative effects on the baby's growth and the length of pregnancy. If a mother is experiencing a lot of stress during pregnancy, it can also affect the baby's future physical and mental health and general development. It can also cause behavioral issues in childhood. Stress in pregnancy also has negative effects on the neurodevelopment of the child.

The immune system

Stress and anxiety release a hormone called cortisol in the body. The effects of cortisol are that it can decrease the immune system's effectiveness. Cortisol causes the functionality of the immune system to become less effective in fighting off infections. It lowers the number of lymphocytes present in the blood and interferes with normal white blood cell communication. When a person experiences an extended period of anxiety, the autonomic nervous system accepts the heightened level of stress as normal.

So, it continues to make a higher level of stress hormones normally. Even after a stressful event has passed, the sympathetic nervous system still produces the same level of hormones because it is the new normal. It is also possible that until a person practices mindfulness or other techniques, the production of the hormones does not go back to normal.

The increased production of these hormones continues to affect the immune system. When the immune system gets weaker, a repetitive cycle is made, which makes it harder to deal with infections.

Chapter 9

How does emotional health affect physical health?

Descartes famously wrote: 'I think, therefore, I am. This saying can also be referred to as, "I move, therefore I think".

Neuropsychology proves that our thoughts are governed by our emotions, which are grounded in our bodies. The mind and body are often perceived as two separate entities, but it is not true. The mind and body are closely related. So mental and physical health are also closely related.

Good mental health positively affects physical health and poor mental health has negative effects on physical health. Studies have found that positive psychological well-being can reduce the risks of heart attacks and strokes. Poor mental health leads to poor physical health and harmful behaviors. Poor psychological well-being can disrupt the ability to think clearly, hindering the ability to make healthy decisions. Neglecting mental well-being can lead to severe health conditions and health problems.

The brain and body are connected through neural pathways, which include neurotransmitters, hormones, and chemicals. These neural pathways transmit signals between the body and the brain and help us control our everyday functions ranging from breathing, digestion, and pain sensations to movement, thinking, and feeling. Emotional responses are not only limited to the brain but also extend to the endocrine and immune systems. They are also organs and have emotional responses.

These organs have common chemical languages, and they are constantly communicating with one another. Therefore, whatever happens in the brain also affects the body, as there is constant communication exchanged between the two. This communication happens through chemical and physical messengers, such as hormones and neurotransmitters. Researchers have identified the actual neural network that connects the cerebral cortex to the adrenal medulla, which activates the body's response in stressful situations.

In order to understand the mind-body connection, it is important to understand that this happens because of the feedback loop between the body and the brain. This means that the brain gives feedback to the body and the body also signals the brain. Feelings are not restricted to emotions, but they also imply physical sensations.

Feelings are bodily experiences, and all feelings have bodily sensations that define them. For example, when you feel nervous, you might feel it in your gut. Your heart rate goes up, and your posture can also change from open to closed. When you feel confident, you feel relaxed, and you stand up tall. Your breath and heart rate also becomes relaxed.

The knowledge that there is a connection between mind and body is not new. Until approximately 300 years ago, all systems of medicine throughout the world treated the mind and body. But during the 17th century, the western world saw the mind and body as two separate entities. According to this view, the mind is the thoughts, and the body is a machine that has no connection to the mind.

These viewpoints add some benefits, and it has acted as a foundation for advancement in surgery and pharmaceutical care. But it has also reduced scientific inquiry into human emotions and spiritual life. In the 20th century, this view gradually changed as researchers studied the mind and body connection and started to scientifically show the links between mind and body.

The mind-body connection is important to understanding and dealing with anxiety. It is impossible to recover from anxiety if we deny that the mind has an influence on the body and vice versa. Physical and emotional health are connected. Therefore, you can treat one by reading the other. By using mind-body concepts, it is possible to improve treatment plans and mind-body therapies can also provide you with valuable tools for your recovery from anxiety.

Anxiety can lead to psychosomatic disorders

If you have ever felt physically ill, and you have found no explanation for your physical discomforts, then it is possible that what you are experiencing is a psychosomatic disorder. It is very common for people to ignore the symptoms of anxiety. Some people suffering from anxiety think that it is a behavioral fault, so they do not seek any medical help or attention. But anxiety has ways of manifesting itself in physical disorders if we leave it untreated. Undiagnosed anxiety can lead to psychosomatic disorders.

Scientists believe that stress releases hormones and chemicals in the body, which are stress hormones and can cause psychosomatic symptoms. During stressful moments, our body releases hormones like adrenaline and cortisol. These hormones are helpful for our fight-or-flight response.

When we feel stressed, they help us quickly get on our feet. A kind of stress which is called "eustress" refers to positive stress that motivates people to do stuff. But the continuous release of these hormones can cause a lot of physical symptoms like digestive issues, heart issues, blood pressure, shortness of breath, and chest pain, and it can also manifest as psychosomatic symptoms.

Stress hormones that are released when the body experiences stressful situations also cause fluctuations in serotonin levels, which weaken our immune system. It increases the chances of catching an infection and worsens our physical ailments, which are already present. Psychosomatic disorder explains the relationship between the mind and the body. Psychosomatic is a term that is a combination of the Greek words psyche, meaning mind and somatic, meaning body. Psychosomatic disorders make it clearer that the mind and body are linked. Human health depends on the health of both the mind and the body.

Psychosomatic disorder

Psychosomatic disorder is a condition in which psychological stresses affect somatic functioning to the point of distress. Somatic functioning is the physiological functioning of the body. Psychosomatic disorder is a condition of dysfunction or structural damage in physical organs. It results because of inappropriate activation of the involuntary nervous system and the biochemical response. Psychosomatic disorder is a psychological condition that leads to physical symptoms.

These physical symptoms often have no medical explanation. Psychosomatic disorders can affect almost all parts of the body. People who suffer from psychosomatic disorders seek frequent medical attention, but they do not get any diagnosis. They may have excessive thoughts, feelings, or concerns about their symptoms. This affects their ability to function well in daily life. People suffering from psychosomatic disorders are often unaware of their anxiety. So, they do not report any psychological frustration or distress.

Psychosomatic disorder is also known as somatic symptom disorder, somatic symptoms, or somatic pain. The exchange between the conscious mind and the unconscious mind, which carries repressed sadness, hurt, emotional pain, and anger, is important.

If this exchange is disrupted, or if the conscious and subconscious mind has disagreement, that is when psychosomatic symptoms become more conscious. If our core need for expressing our repressed feelings and anxiety is ignored, then the body holds all the tension inside, which manifests as psychosomatic disorders.

Statistics of psychosomatic disorder

Psychosomatic disorder is very common. According to a survey, 5% to 7% of the general population suffer from symptoms of psychosomatic disorders. Research has also proven that women have somatic pain about 10 times more than men, but the reason behind this is still unknown.

We experience some psychosomatic symptoms from time to time, but it does not mean that you suffer from a psychosomatic disorder. It is common to feel some psychosomatic symptoms such as palpitations, sweating, and some other symptoms. If you are experiencing a stressful situation, all of us can relate to feeling butterflies in our stomachs before we give a presentation or speak to our boss about a difficult situation.

Triggers of Psychosomatic Disorder

Anyone can develop a psychosomatic disorder. Any kind of mental or psychological disorder which is left untreated and undiagnosed can manifest itself as somatic pain. People of any age can suffer from somatic pain. Some triggers of somatic symptoms can be a chaotic lifestyle, childhood neglect, a history of sexual abuse, physical abuse, or psychological conditions such as anxiety, depression, personality disorders, etc.

Having a history of anxiety or depression can also result in psychosomatic disorders. It is also possible to develop these symptoms if you have experienced a recent traumatic event. It is also possible for childhood trauma to appear at later ages as a psychosomatic disorder. Research has proven that some people seem to have a genetic propensity to be more sensitive to somatic experiences. I have seen in my research that somatic disorders can be inherited.

Symptoms of psychosomatic disorder

If anxiety manifests itself as a psychosomatic disorder, then it can affect almost all parts of the body. The psychosomatic disorder can be evident as fatigue, insomnia, indescribable pains and aches, high blood pressure, trouble breathing, headaches, migraines, indigestion, stomach ulcers or skin rash.

Besides all the physical symptoms of the psychosomatic disorder such as pain and upset stomach, people with the psychosomatic disorder also have other problems and symptoms. It is very common for people suffering from psychosomatic disorder to become angry or irritable at small matters. They believe their medical needs are not being met, whereas there is no medical explanation for their physical pain. It becomes easy for them to diagnose the cause of their pain, which leads them to be angry and irritable.

Psychosomatic disorder can also cause a person to become more anxious, which results in a vicious cycle as anxiety causes psychosomatic disorders and the symptoms of psychosomatic disorder enhance anxiety and negative thoughts.

People suffering from psychosomatic disorders also have difficulties functioning in their daily lives, because they suffer from pain that has no explanation. Some more common symptoms of psychosomatic disorders are muscle paralysis and non-epileptic seizures, which are also known as pseudo-seizures. This is the most severe end of psychosomatic pain.

The symptoms of a psychosomatic disorder can vary from person to person, and it is also possible for these symptoms to change from day to day or year to year. It is also possible for psychosomatic symptoms to overlap with serious health conditions, so it is very important to visit a healthcare provider and rule out serious health conditions before labeling your pain as a psychosomatic symptom.

Chapter 10

How to deal with the physical effects of anxiety

Our bodies are well equipped to handle a small amount of stress. They are remarkably capable of doing so, but when the stress becomes chronic and long-term, it starts to manifest in our physical health. It affects the body in many negative ways. Stress affects all systems of our body, including the musculoskeletal system, respiratory system, cardiovascular system, nervous system, reproductive system, endocrine system, and gastrointestinal system.

It is possible to overcome stress-related illnesses. The first step is to acknowledge that stress not only affects the emotional state but also the physical state of the body. There are various steps to deal with the physical problems of anxiety, and some easy ones are:

Regular exercise: It is possible to beat the level of stress hormones like cortisol levels through exercise. When we exercise, our body releases feel-good hormones such as endorphins which helps to improve mood, sleep, and stress. Physical activities can help people relieve tension. Breathing exercises and all other relaxation techniques can also help calm down the body and mind.

Getting enough sleep: If the body does not get enough sleep, the mind clouds over, and physical health is also affected. Therefore, avoid caffeinated drinks as much as possible after the evening and comfortably ease into sleep at night. If you get enough sleep, it will help you improve your overall well-being. It is a personal experience that on the days on which I have good and undisturbed sleep, I function better and feel less stressed compared to days I have not slept well. So, it is very important to get a healthy amount of sleep, to deal with the physical effects of anxiety.

Interact with people: Humans are social animals, and we crave social interactions. We are not meant to live alone. We interact with people and loved ones. It helps to clear our mental fog, which is caused because of anxiety. No one has to go through the negative effects of anxiety alone. It is OK to take help from other people. When we are unable to see the positive side of life, our loved ones can show us the beauty of life and it can make it easier for us to deal with negative effects of anxiety. If you are feeling anxious and you feel that your negative thoughts are taking over, take some time out to talk to loved ones. It will help make you feel better. Studies have found that interaction with friends and family members produces oxytocin in women. Oxytocin is a happy hormone, and it can fight off anxiety. It is also referred to as a "natural stress reliever."

Learn to Say NO! If you can't then get my book, Unfuck Your Poor Boundaries. Although it is important to interact with people and go out to meet people. It is also important to know that it is ok to keep your limitations in taking responsibility and learning to say no. Learning to say "no" helps you manage your anxiety as it reduces stressors. You don't have to feel obliged to say yes to everything people ask for. It is something that develops from early childhood.

If we are used to pleasing our parents or caregivers at an early age, then we become people pleasers and we try to do everything people ask us to do in order to make them happy. But it is important to identify this pattern and learn to say no because we do not need to add more burden on ourselves than we can handle.

Learn to Stay Mindful: Staying mindful helps to decrease the symptoms of anxiety and depression. If you are experiencing anxiety-induced effects of negative thinking, then mindfulness can help you combat them. There are various ways of staying mindful. Some of them are yoga or meditation. It also helps to write about what you are stressed about. It is an excellent approach to managing stress. It enables you to identify the stressors in your life so you can do something positive about them.

Distract yourself: if you think that the root of your physical symptoms is anxiety, distraction can help you deal with these symptoms. If you distract your mind, it can help you distract your focus away from your physical problems. Distracting yourself can help you combat increased anxiety and its negative physical symptoms. When we move our body from one activity to another, we take our mind off our symptoms, and it helps us feel better. Distractions can be different for different people. You can try different activities to figure out which is better to make your mind calmer.

Grounding techniques

The grounding technique is a practice that can help people pull away from flashbacks, unwanted memories, and negative emotions. Grounding techniques are exercises that help you refocus on the present moment to distract yourself from your anxious thoughts and the feelings resulting from such anxious thoughts. Grounding techniques can create space for distressing feelings in different situations. They are an easy and effective way to deal with the effects of anxiety. Grounding techniques can help people deal with distressing feelings which are caused by anxiety, stress, depression, mood, post-traumatic stress disorder, and dissociation.

Even in my personal experience with anxiety, I have found grounding techniques to be the most helpful way to deal with negative thoughts. Anxiety takes a person away from reality, and the brain becomes forged. A person who is suffering from anxiety thinks negatively and excessively. Anxiety can also cause people to create situations in their heads that are trauma-inducing. Anxiety takes a person away from the actual reality and immerses a person in a dramatic fake reality, which makes the situation worse. Grounding techniques help bring the person back to reality, so they can realize that the traumatic situation was in their mind and, in reality, they are safe.

Grounding techniques use the five senses of touch, smell, taste, hearing, and sight to bring a person back to reality. Grounding techniques also use tangible objects, things that you can touch, to help you cope with distress. Grounding techniques use tools, such as visualization and senses, to distract the person from negative feelings and thoughts. Ignoring a panic attack or a traumatic flashback can easily take over physical responses. It becomes difficult to focus on the present moment, but grounding techniques can help a person focus on the present and return the brain and feelings to a place of safety.

Touch something near you

An important grounding technique that can be used is to touch something near you. Touching something and focusing on its texture and feeling, whether the thing is soft, hard, light, warm, or cool, can help people ground themselves back to reality. It can also help to think of specific colors and try to find things around yourself in those colors. It also helps to put your hands in water; focusing on the water's temperature and how it feels on your fingertips, your palms, and the back of your hands can also help. You can use warm water first and then cold. Focusing on how it feels to switch from the temperature of the water can also help deal with negative thoughts by bringing a person back to reality. You can also touch a piece of ice and feel how it melts on your palm. Focusing on the sensation can also help you ground yourself back into reality.

Breathing exercises

It also helps to focus on your breathing if you are feeling anxious. Focus on your inhaling and exhaling. If it helps, you can also number your breath and count them. Allow yourself to feel how your breath fills your lungs and focus on your breathing. Deep inhaling and exhaling can also help in grounding. Focus on breathing techniques can also be enhanced by placing hands on the abdomen and watching your hands move up and down with your breath. Breathing techniques are an effective strategy for returning to the present.

Change your position

It also helps to change your posture or change your position if you have been in the same position for a long time. If you have been sitting, standing up will help you, and if you have been standing up for a long time, then setting might help you. By changing your posture, the brain focuses on muscle movement, and it relieves anxious thoughts. You can also take a short walk and concentrate on your steps. You can also count them. Notice the rhythm of your footsteps and how it feels to put your foot on the ground and lift it back again. Doing a few stretches or light jogging can also help.

The 5-4-3-2-1 method

The 5-4-3-2-1 method is a technique which I have personal experience with. During the worst episodes of my anxiety, I used this method to ground myself. I found that this was the easiest method as it did not require any prompts and did not even require me to change my position, as it is something that can appear very difficult if you are experiencing anxiety.

Practicing this method activates all 5 senses, and this helps the brain focus back on reality. This method uses the five senses to notice things around you, working backward from 5 to 1. You need to list five things you hear, four things you can see, three things you can touch, two things you can smell, and one thing you can taste. You can attempt to notice small things which you rarely pay attention to, and it will help you in gaining back your control.

Mental grounding techniques

Mental grounding techniques use mental distractions to help redirect thoughts away from distressing feelings and bring them back to the present. Mental grounding techniques may include playing a memory game, like looking at a detailed photograph or picture for five to 10 seconds. Then turn the photograph upside down and try to recreate it in your mind with as much detail as possible.

Or you can use even trickier methods, such as solving a mental equation. If you are not much of a math person, then you can recite something like a poem, song, or anything which you know by heart. You can recite it quickly or in your head.

Saying these words will help your mind focus on the words, and if you say them aloud, your brain will also focus on muscle movement resulting from moving your mouth and lips. It also helps to visualize a daily task you enjoy doing, such as, when I feel panicked, I visualize packing my suitcase for a long vacation. I imagined all the things that I would take with me, and I mentally packed my suitcase. This helps me tremendously.

If you think that you are not being present in reality because you're distracted from memories of the past, then you can use different strategies. Some of them include focusing on a recent event, such as a to-do list for the day. Focusing on future events, particularly your goals, ambitions, or dreams, can also help. If you are feeling unsafe and anxiety is making you feel as if you're about to experience harm, then you should remind yourself of your current safety. List at least 5 things in your environment that makes you feel safe.

Researchers have observed that grounded participants experience an improvement in their mood compared to ungrounded people. Some people also refer to grounding as "earthing."

Kick anxiety's ass – Effective steps

These are some powerful steps to combat anxiety. These steps will help you tremendously in your life.

Step 1: take a breath, but a deep breath, as deep as you can through your mouth, and hold it for as long as you can. You might feel a little dizzy. It's normal. Then, when you can't hold it anymore, exhale out your nose. It is important that you exhale out of your nose and not your mouth. You will feel instantly calm.

Step 2: Assess your environment. If you are honest with yourself, do you truly see a threat in your environment? In most cases, there will be no immediate threat and what you feel is the fear of there being a threat. Tell yourself immediately, "I am safe. I am in control. I am safe. I am only feeling old feelings from the past", and keep repeating it at least 10 times. When you do this, just the thought of being safe will trigger a positive biochemical reaction in your body, and it will respond as though it is now safe.

Step 3: You will normally feel either the freeze instinctive response or the running away instinct, also known as flight. Here, if you are in a public place, take these 2 steps and then jump up and down, shake your hands, body, and legs. This will immediately discharge the nervous energy that is stuck in your autonomic nervous system. You will feel calm immediately.

Step 4: In your mind, affirm the following affirmation, "I call my power back from this anxiety," and repeat it at least 3 times. You will feel a powerful shift in your emotional body.

Chapter 11 Affirmations

I call my power back from times when I felt unsupported.

I call my power back from people who challenged me.

I call my power back from times when I felt unsafe.

I call my power back from times when I felt ignored.

I call my power back from times when I felt unheard.

I call my power back from times when I felt invisible.

I acknowledge the difference between my identity and my mother's anxiety.

I acknowledge the difference between my identity and my father's anxiety.

I acknowledge the difference between my identity and the anxiety that I took that belongs to other people.

I acknowledge the difference between my identity and feeling unworthy. Who I am is worthy of creating the life that I want.

I acknowledge the difference between my identity and giving up who I am is strong.

I am capable and intelligent. Any fears or doubts that you have are releasing, drifting away.

I acknowledge the difference between my identity and feeling stuck.

I am a powerful driving force, achieving my goals and creating opportunities.

I acknowledge the difference between my identity and anxiety.

I call my power back from times when I felt overwhelmed.

I reclaim my birthright to be and feel safe.

I reclaim my birthright to be and feel supported.

I reclaim my birthright to be and feel peaceful.

I reclaim my inner balance.

I reclaim my inner peace.

I reclaim my inner happiness.

Chapter 12

Understanding hidden messages in your body relating to anxiety

This exercise is designed to help you to find hidden messages behind your current emotional stress and even physical pain. Your body is talking, are you listening?

It is well known that our emotional stress can show up in our body through tension, pain, discomfort, and even ailments. Each emotion has its own impact on the body and our health. Negative emotions create stress and physiological changes in the body.

Each negative emotion holds its own influence and impact on the body. For example, sometimes you might be so angry that you get a headache. We store emotional stress in certain parts of our body. Meaning if we energize a certain emotion long enough, it can affect a certain part of our body.

Our head, for example, psychosomatically relates to control. So, if there are circumstances in your life that cause you to feel out of control, anger and frustration, you might get a headache. If you have a lot of responsibility to deal with, you might notice your shoulders and backache, as we store emotional burdens and responsibility there.

Awareness of a problem is a problem half solved. When you have awareness of which unresolved emotion is hampering your health and quality of life, you can apply the correct tool manage the problem. We often fail our bodies by not understanding its language and therefore, we often apply the wrong tool to deal with the challenge. Sometimes these "tools" we use are coping mechanisms such as drinking, smoking and many more bad habits which does not directly resolve the stress we are feeling in the body.

Let's dive into influential theory to build and expand a powerful understanding of your body and its language.

What if you feel pain or discomfort but don't have an ailment or injury? What's next? I call this psychosomatic tension, pain, discomfort, sensations, or heaviness. I have studied it for 15 years and worked with over 6,000 people all over the world. When the body hurts, it sends a powerful message. It's telling you it has reached its limit. That is what my work, Metaphysical Anatomy Volume 1 and 3, is all about! Volume 2 is a powerful healing technique behind my research. There are they reveal over 679 medical ailments and accurate hidden emotional messages and stress revealed in Volume 1 and 3! But how does it work?

Tension, pain, discomfort, sensations, or heaviness is a way for your body to communicate to you. It's telling you it has reached its threshold, coping with a suppressed emotion.

Have you ever noticed that when things are going really well in your life, you don't pay attention to your body? But suddenly when we feel sick or have tension, pain, discomfort, sensations, or heaviness in the body, then we pay attention. Sometimes we have strong negative emotions which are running in our subconscious mind that can greatly influence the body's health. We feel the anxiety, pain, discomfort, sensations, or heaviness, but we don't understand the source.

We don't always notice how our bodies are weakening when we're in a state of euphoria or "autopilot," until our gut starts acting up. This is because of all the stress. Your immune system might feel so weak that you catch the flu, get bronchitis, or get headaches. Maybe you're not drinking enough water.

Stress triggers tension, pain, discomfort, sensations, or heaviness in the body. A lot of mental and physical ideas about pain and stress are the same. Both pain and stress upset the body's homeostasis and make it decide to help it adapt to its surroundings, especially when you don't listen to its messages. It is also forced to adapt to what it can if it does not have the resources needed to function optimally. How can the body function at its optimal capacity? If we learn to listen to it and its messages. Both chronic stress and chronic pain share the same behavioral pattern, which stems from unresolved negative emotional memories. These memories can be from an injury, accident, or emotional trauma.

Most of us have to deal with stress every day. The effects it has on our lives may be different for each person, but they are there, whether they are short-term or long-term. Diseases, viruses, and infections are treated because we know they can harm us. Stress is not a virus, an infection, or a disease, but does that mean it can't harm us? Stress may not be a disease in and of itself, but it can cause both physical and mental problems. So, let's talk about stress and how it can cause psychosomatic tension, pain, discomfort, sensations, or heaviness in the body.

The mind-body link: Most of the time, we think of stress as just a way of thinking. Stress stems from past trauma, career, relationship, friendship challenges, and the list goes on. Most people think that stress only affects their minds because it is how they think and see things, right? No, not the case. Then how can someone say that stress can cause pain, discomfort, sensations or heaviness in the body when they feel stressed sometimes? Does stress only cause this in the mind, or can it also cause pain and discomfort in the body? Our minds and bodies are closely linked!

We are a mix of these two elements. In the same way, our minds and bodies work together to keep us alive. Because of this, stress has adverse effects not only on our mental health but also on our physical health.

Neuropsychology says that our bodies are the physical basis for both how we feel and how we think. Even though most people think of the mind and body as two separate things, they are actually very connected. As a result, there is a strong link between your mental and physical health. When your mental health is good, it helps your physical health. When your mental health is bad, it can harm your physical health. Studies show that if you have a healthy mindset, you are less likely to get a long-term illness like a heart attack or stroke. If a person's mental health isn't good, it can make it harder for them to feel positive, think clearly, and make good decisions. If you don't take care about your mental health, you could end up with health problems.

Neurotransmitters, hormones, and other chemicals make up neural networks, which connect the brain and the rest of the body. These connections between neurons help us control many things in the body, like breathing, moving, feeling pain, thinking, making decisions, and feeling. Emotions don't just affect the brain; they also affect the endocrine system and the immune system. Since the brain and the body are always linked, everything that happens in the brain influences the body.

All of these organs use the same chemical language to talk to each other all the time. The neuronal signals become the way for the brain and the rest of the body to talk to each other. So, anything that happens in the brain affects the body, and the same is true for the body. Hormones and neurotransmitters are the chemical and physical signals that the brain and body use to communicate with each other. Studies have found that the actual neural network that connects the cerebral cortex to the adrenal medulla triggers the body's response to stress, showing that stress not only affects the brain but also causes the body to do things.

To understand the mind-body connection, it's important to know that it happens because the body and brain are connected by a feedback loop. This means that both the body and the brain use signals to talk to each other. Feelings are more than just emotions; they also include sensations in the body. Because feelings are physical experiences, they all have specific body sensations that can be used to describe them.

When you're stressed, for example, your blood pressure goes up, your heart rate goes up, you might start to sweat, and your posture might change from open to closed. But when you're calm and sure of yourself, you stand tall, and your heart rate and breathing slow down. It is well known that the mind and body are connected.

Before about 300 years ago, all medical systems looked at the body and mind as a whole. But people in the West began to see that the mind and body were two separate things. From this point of view, the body is a machine that has nothing to do with the mind, and the mind is made up of thoughts. Both of these points of view have helped improve medicine and surgery.

But it has also slowed down scientific research into spirituality and emotions, like how feelings like anxiety, stress, and nervousness can cause pain, discomfort, sensations or heaviness in the body. Over the course of the 20th century, this view started to change as scientists started to look into the connection between the mind and the body and show evidence of these links. Results showed that our physical, mental, and psychological systems, as well as our physical and mental pain and health, are all connected.

The mind-body connection is important for understanding and dealing with pain because we can't get better from stress-related pain if we don't believe that the mind can affect the body and vice versa.

Since mental and physical health are linked, you can use information from one to figure out and treat the other. Mind-body principles can be used to improve treatment plans, and mind-body treatments can give you tools to help you deal with pain caused by many things.

Our bodies and minds are two sides of the same coin. Our physical health and well-being are connected to our mental health and well-being. Even though stress seems to cause only emotional and mental pain, it has an obvious impact on our physical health.

Pain and stress: People often think that "pain, discomfort, sensations or heaviness in the body" only means physical pain or not being physically well. That is only if you are not able to pinpoint the exact sensation you are feeling and where in your body you are feeling it.

However, mental and emotional pain are just as serious as physical pain, and mental and emotional health are just as important as physical health. Physical and mental health are both important for a person to live a healthy, happy, and successful life. Even though stress is usually thought of as a state of mental tension and difficulty, it has effects on our lives that are not just mental. It can cause pain and other physical problems as well.

Some of the most common and serious effects of stress are insomnia, anxiety, restlessness, trouble making decisions, feelings of anger, loss of confidence, irritability, short temper, etc. When stress lasts for a long time, it makes mental health problems more likely. It can also make you feel sad and worried. Stress can also make you feel moody, helpless, hopeless, unhappy, unstable, agitated, irritable, and unable to relax or calm down. It can lead to even worse mental health problems, like depression, anxiety, burnout, or even panic attacks. It has a big effect on how we feel, how we act, and how healthy we are. Stress that comes from a traumatic event could even lead to post-traumatic stress disorder (PTSD). PTSD is a mental health condition that can be caused by seeing or experiencing a traumatic event. It can have serious effects on a person's health and day-to-day life, which can't be ignored.

If a person is exposed to intense and ongoing stressors during their formative years, they are more likely to develop anxiety and mood disorders, issues with losing control of their anger, hypo-immune dysfunction, medical morbidity, and structural changes in their central nervous system.

Our central nervous system (CNS) doesn't make isolated responses; instead, it makes responses that are both mental and physical for every stimulus. When there is an immediate fight-or-flight situation, mammals tend to have more hormonal and autonomic activity, which makes it easier for their muscles to work. Also, stress has more than one impact on our physical health. Aside from the fact that stress affects the way our bodies work. It affects our minds, stress is also causing many physical diseases and health problems.

For instance, stress can cause high blood pressure, heartburn, headaches, stomach problems, and pain in the muscles.

Here is the catch!

Stress is not just stress; it is there because of unresolved negative emotions we feel. Just holding a negative thought can cause stress. Everyday day you have 95 000 thoughts more or less.

Then 75 000 (who is counting right) of those thoughts are repeated the next day. It is shown that we think negative thoughts much more than positive thoughts.

So, by repeating these conscious and subconscious thoughts, we are building and building on top of our stressed mindset. Now, thoughts stem from what? They stem from emotions and how certain people and circumstances made us feel, which we never fully addressed and resolved.

Have you noticed how certain negative emotions are connected to certain tension, pain, discomfort, heaviness, or ailments in the body?

Recognizing This Phenomenon

It's strange how emotions work. Both love and heartbreak happen in your mind, but they feel very different in the body. On the other hand, excitement and fear are two very different feelings that almost feel the same. Even more complicated is the fact that feelings are personal, so it's hard to tell if other people feel the same way you do. This new study by a group of Finns is so interesting because they have figured out where in the body most people feel emotions. It turns out that most of us feel our emotions in the same places and this is what I have discovered myself with my research and working with thousands of people and documented this research in Metaphysical Anatomy Volume 1 and 3. Volume 2 is a powerful healing technique behind my research.

Neuroscientist Lauri Nummenmaa of the University of Turku in Finland and a team of three other Finnish researchers have been working on this question since at least 2014. In 2014, they published a smaller body map that showed where 14 "basic" and "non-basic" emotions (like "happiness" and "pride") were felt in the body. In 2015, they also made a map of the places people let others touch them based on their relationship with them. This map showed that the places people let others touch them were very similar across cultures. But for this new study, they pulled out all the stops to map an amazing 100 different feelings. These feelings fell into seven groups: cognition, like thinking and reasoning; sensation and perception, like seeing and hearing; homeostatic states, like hunger and thirst; physiological processes, like sleeping and breathing; feelings related to illness, like coughing and fever; and feelings related to psychiatric disorders, like depression and anxiety.

Over the course of three experiments, the team found more than 1,000 people to take part. In the first, people rated how much each feeling happens in their body versus in their mind, how good each one feels, and how much control they have over it. In the second, people had to report how similar their feelings were. For example, you might put guilt and stress next to each other and love and pride far away. The results of that experiment placed emotions into five groups: positive feelings, negative feelings, cognitive processes, somatic (or physical) states and illnesses, and homeostatic states (bodily functions).

In the last experiment, participants were given one feeling at a time along with a blank outline of a human body, and asked to color the part of the body where they felt the feeling. Then, they put all of this information together to make 100 "body sensation maps" that showed where these feelings were felt.

Some of the places were not surprising. For example, hunger is felt in the stomach, thirst in the throat, and thinking and remembering are done in the head. But some were more surprising, even though they seemed to make sense. Positive emotions like gratitude and togetherness looked a lot alike, as did negative emotions like guilt and despair. Feelings were mapped in the heart, head, and stomach in that order. Another pair of opposite emotions that were felt all over the body were mania and exhaustion. "Self-regulation," which you might not expect to feel, was felt in the head and hands. This might be because controlling your impulses often comes down to controlling what your hands do.

The Subconscious Mind and Emotions

The body is a record of everything we've ever done. We can learn more about how stuck emotions and physical illnesses cause us to suffer as we connect the mind, body, and spirit. We can go years, if not decades, without realizing we have trapped emotions or where they came from. We end up holding on to the energy that is blocked, which can lead to pain or psychosomatic tension, discomfort, or heaviness in the body.

When traumatic events aren't dealt with in a conscious way, they can cause chronic fear, stress, and even PTSD. Chronic anxiety, anger, and grief are often stored in the body. This can cause muscle tension, which can lead to fibromyalgia, digestive problems, mental illnesses, and more severe ailments.

Psychological tension is any feeling of worry, frustration, sadness, or anger that comes from how we see things. When we have a negative, fearful, or blame-finding attitude, our muscles tend to hold more tension.

How Emotions Affect Our Bodies

Everything that exists on the physical plane is a result of something that exists on the Metaphysical plane. Scientists are now able to measure how different emotional states affect the body. Depending on how you feel, your body actually gets weaker or stronger.

The lowest vibration is shame, followed by guilt, apathy, grief, fear, anxiety, craving, anger, and hate. On the other hand, things that make you stronger are trust, optimism, willingness, acceptance, forgiveness, understanding, love, reverence, joy, peace, and enlightenment. Have you been hurt or hurt yourself? What was going on in your life back then? Think back to how you were thinking and how you felt.

When an accident happens, injuries will more likely take place in the psychosomatic area where resembling the emotional stress you have been energizing consciously or subconsciously. Your biology is a mix of how your mental, physical, and emotional states work together or against each other. For example, the left side of your body shows unresolved challenges with femininity, mother figure, spirituality, and so forth. While the right side shows unresolved stress associated with masculinity, decision making, father figures and so forth. There can be a theme where pain or injuries usually take place on just one side of the body.

Why do we store emotions in the body?

Scientists are finding more and more proof of what ancient healing practices have known for a long time, which is that the body stores emotions. The mind, the body, and how we see the world are all inextricably linked. Think about the last time you were angry, and pay attention to how it made you feel in your body.

Whether you were aware of it or not, you probably clenched your teeth, tightened your jaw, creased your brow, and clenched your fists.

Now, think back to a time when you felt sad. Your upper body may have fallen in and forward. You might remember that the space around your upper chest in front felt really tight. If you've ever cried, you might remember feeling like you couldn't breathe in your throat and chest, and your lungs might have twitched as the tears fell.

These strong emotions and so many others, like traumatic events, are felt and shown in the body in a way that can't be denied. They can also get stuck in the body because we are often taught to hold back our feelings, keep our mouths shut, hide our anger and grief, and not put our need for pleasure first. Instead of letting emotions, which are just moving energy, move through our bodies, we end up letting them build up in certain parts of the body, which can lead to pain and other physical problems.

Negative emotions can make your body release a lot of hormones that make your heartbeat fast, your breathing shallow, your muscles tense up, and so on. Positive feelings can make you feel warm, tingly, or even give you butterflies in your stomach.

For example, the DongUiBoGam says, "The liver controls anger, the heart controls happiness, the spleen controls thoughtfulness, the lungs control sadness, and the kidneys control fear." The numbering of the words used to describe the connections between emotions and body parts

Researchers have found that the gut and the brain are closely linked. This link is important not only for handling emotions and stress, but also for helping digestion. The gut is where emotions are felt, especially emotional stress, with your closest relatives. In the gut, you can feel things like sadness, anger, nervousness, fear, and joy.

Where does the body store trauma?

Childhood trauma can affect the mental and physical development of children and teens for the rest of their lives. Let's look at what happens to our body and mind after we've been through stressful or traumatic event.

How do you define emotional information?

It's very important to show how you feel. Experts think that our emotions can tell our bodies to "fight," "flee," or "freeze" when we feel threatened. When we feel negative emotions like fear and stress, our bodies react the most. This is because these emotions can keep us safe in dangerous situations. But the feelings don't always go away after the event is over. These feelings turn into information about how we feel, and they can turn into thoughts based on a compilation of memories which stays in our bodies as unresolved trauma. So where do these bad feelings live in our bodies?

Emotional information is stored in our organs, tissues, skin, and muscles in the form of "packages." These "packages" let the emotional information stay in our body parts until we can "release" it. Negative emotions, in particular, have effects on the body that last for a long time.

Here are some examples that show how our bodies understand how we feel: When we are angry, scared, or worried, our chests, backs, and upper bodies do more work. This makes our muscles tighten up and makes our heartbeat faster.

When we feel love and happiness, it spreads through our whole bodies. These feelings help the body in a good way. They lower the risk of heart disease, lower blood pressure, help you sleep better, and can even make your diet better.

Your liver is hurt by anger. Fear can make your kidneys hurt. Your lungs are changed by grief. Your heart is affected by unresolved anger related to boundary failures. When you worry, your stomach can hurt.

These are all stress points. But when you take a closer look, you will notice that each stress point is driven and caused by an underlying unresolved pain point in your life. So where do these feelings we don't want to feel go? They become stuck in our body. How? Because you energize these negative thoughts and emotions consciously and subconsciously without resolving them with the right "tools".

Strange Pains and Aches

I've been studying where people keep their bad feelings for a long time. Surely, not all body pains or illnesses are caused by the mind. But as I looked at how people's bodies react to stress, I noticed patterns.

Let's look at repression that is healthy vs. not healthy. Repression is caused by fear, which usually has its roots in your past. Repression is often necessary, especially when you feel too much or go through a traumatic event. But relying too much on repression can lead to psychosomatic symptoms and patterns of self-harm.

Pain and Psychosomatic Pain

Even though there are different kinds of pain, the nervous system always uses the same way to deal with it. But when the pain is very bad, the blood pressure goes back to normal quickly. It doesn't mean that acute pain doesn't cause high blood pressure, but because acute pain goes away more quickly, the rise in blood pressure caused by it also goes away and returns to normal more quickly.

On the other hand, when chronic pain happens, blood pressure stays high, and the body's ability to bring blood pressure back to normal is weakened. This can cause more pain, high blood pressure, and a rise in the number of people with heart disease. So, chronic pain makes blood pressure go up even more and makes it hard to bring it back down to normal levels.

How does the nervous system pick up on and make sense of pain?

The brain is one of the most amazing things that people are still trying to figure out. We are always amazed by how well the living brain works together. How does the brain know the difference between a feather's touch and a pinch? This is something to think about. Also, how does the brain know when the body hurts?

When we think about the connection between the nervous system and the pain in the body, we might have a lot of questions. How does the brain know when we are hurting? If the signals don't get to the brain, what happens? Then we shouldn't feel any pain, right? How does the body know when a certain part of the body needs to express pain? Does the brain send signals to the body to tell it if the pain is going to be short-term or long-term? All of these questions seem very difficult, but it is possible to figure out how to answer them.

The brain and nerves: First off, you should know what the nervous system is and how it works. The nervous system is made up of two main parts. The brain and spinal cord are these parts. The central nervous system is made up of these two parts. The peripheral nervous system is made up of nerves that send and receive information. Our bodies have ways to talk to us.

Each part of the body is always talking to the other parts, which is what makes the body function. Nerves send messages to the brain and spinal cord about different parts of the body. The brain and spinal cord also send signals to the muscles that move our legs, arms, and back. Sensors that measure how flexible, strong, and durable our muscles are constantly sending information to the spinal cord. Through the spinal cord, sensory nerves and impulses send information to the brain, and the brain sends information to the motor nerves.

So, this is why we can do most things. Let's look at a real-life example of something that can happen to us. When we put our hands close to a flame, the spinal cord sends a message to the brain. Then the brain will see it as a threat and a bad situation, and it will send signals to the nerves that control our muscles.

Because of these signals, the muscles in our hands will tighten, and we'll pull our hands away from the flame. Every action we take, from simple ones like picking up a spoon to more complicated ones like running, is the result of this clear communication between the brain and the muscles.

How the Body Stores Pain

A lot can be said about how the body remembers trauma, how it responds to pain, and why it responds to pain in certain ways. There are also a lot of feelings involved. I know that when I'm angry, I can sometimes feel so angry that I can feel the muscles between my shoulder blades. They start to feel like they're getting bigger, and they start to hurt a lot.

When we look at these parts and how stress can affect nerve receptors and how it's sent through the fascia, which is a beautiful part of the tissue or, as most people will say, the largest organ in the body, we can see that it has a lot to do with how pain is spread through the body.

The tricky thing about pain is that when it comes from emotional stress, we can sometimes feel a certain way about it. We have that stress, and we might feel it in our heads or our feet right now. It might be behind our backs.

Now, most of you know my book, "Metaphysical Anatomy Volume 1 and 3," is about psychosomatic, emotional, and stress patterns that are hidden in certain parts of your body. So, if there is tension, pain, discomfort, sensations or heaviness in your body, you will naturally look at the affected area. You can look it up in the book and find out what hidden emotional stress is making this pain worse. In this section, I share a fun shortcut for beginners.

The reason is that stress, that hidden emotional message, is what needs to be recognized. This is what needs to be listened to. This is how the body tries to tell you something. It does not speak in a verbal language like you do. It speaks a different language. It's up to us to adjust to how the body talks to us and the pain, discomfort, sensations, ailments, or heaviness it uses to tell us what's going on.

When we think about the tension, pain, discomfort, sensations, or heaviness caused by emotional stress, we have to remember that emotions are stored all over the body. We don't just store and keep emotions in our minds.

Let's find the answers behind your stress!

So how you find deeper answers behind your current stress? It's actually quite simple. When you observe the challenge, you feel stuck with, always look at the emotional side of it. Meaning? How does this challenge make you feel? When you are aware of the emotional stress, then observe with patience, where in your body do you feel this stress? Meaning? You might feel this emotional stress as tension, tightness, or discomfort in the body. Sometimes you might feel it's nowhere. In that case, observe where your attention feels drawn to intuitively in your body when you think about your emotional challenge.

So here we go. If you have anxiety let's explore deeper unresolve emotional stress behind it.

Step 1: How does your current emotional stress / anxiety make you feel emotionally?

_____

Step 2: Where in your body do you feel or sense it?

_____

Step 3: Once you have your answer, refer to the Quick Reference Guide under Attachment A. There is a short version and slight longer version in a sheet. Read the message regarding possible hidden messages for the answer you wrote at Step 2.

_____

Step 4: Combine answer at Step 1 with answer at Step 3. This will give you the hidden message in your body as to what has been triggered in your subconscious mind.

_____

If you have physical pain hampering you then you have to check out my book "Unfuck Your Pain"

Attachment A - Quick Reference Guide

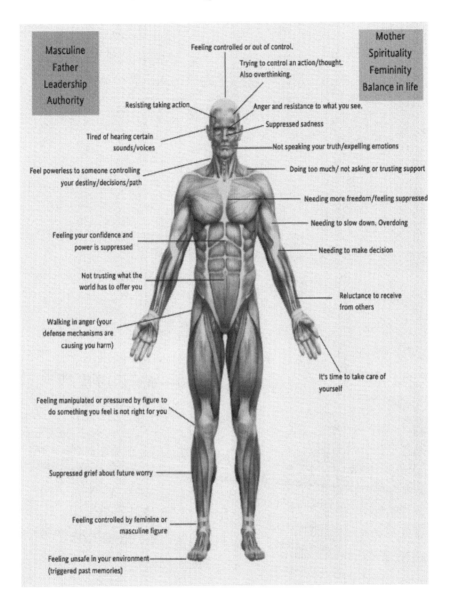

Masculine
Father
Leadership
Authority

Mother
Spirituality
Femininity
Balance in life

Feeling controlled or out of control.

Trying to control an action/thought.
Also overthinking.

Resisting taking action

Anger and resistance to what you see.

Suppressed sadness

Tired of hearing certain
sounds/voices

Not speaking your truth/expelling emotions

Feel powerless to someone controlling
your destiny/decisions/path

Doing too much/ not asking or trusting support

Needing more freedom/feeling suppressed

Needing to slow down. Overdoing

Feeling your confidence and
power is suppressed

Needing to make decision

Not trusting what the
world has to offer you

Reluctance to receive
from others

Walking in anger (your
defense mechanisms are
causing you harm)

It's time to take care of
yourself

Feeling manipulated or pressured by figure to
do something you feel is not right for you

Suppressed grief about future worry

Feeling controlled by feminine or
masculine figure

Feeling unsafe in your environment
(triggered past memories)

Body Part	Possible Key Emotions
Age spots	Skin trauma stemming from ancestry line due to sun exposure. Feeling resentful toward circumstances. Frustration and irritation that has grown out of control.
Ankles	Flexibility related to the future, control issues, stubbornness and conflict with mother.
Anus	Refusal to let go of bad and sabotaging patterns that are still serving you. Holding onto toxic and unhealthy love and relationships.
Arteries	One's ability to give to others and support (fear of giving too much of yourself, fear of being depleted or taken advantage of).
Arms	Fear of being powerful and reclaiming your own personal power and identity.
Back	Support, structure, responsibility, stability.
Middle Back	Feeling responsible for others, blurred line between what is your issue and what is not. Humiliation, embarrassment; feeling dominated and controlled.
Lower Back	Financial responsibilities, other's needs, burdens; feeling under pressure.
Bacteria	Guilt and regret, self-punishment, sabotage.
Bladder	Feeling pissed off with people in authority. Feeling helpless and disempowered to change your circumstances.
Uthera	Drawing power from your feelings of resentment, don't want to let go of toxic relationships. Feel suppressed and resentful

	leading to hardening of the attitude. Feel attacked by loved ones.
Blood	How you feel about your appearance, how you communicate your needs, life force. How protected you feel from the world.
Bones	Needing to be strong, feeling supported, loyalty of others toward you.
Bones broken	Support has been pulled out from under you. Losing control of your life. Fear of change. Sabotaging personal progress. Needing to break away from old habits and take more time to make decisions.
Brain	Control issues, what you see, and feel are not coherent, resulting in conflict. Feeling unable to control what your brain senses, your connection to your environment is traumatic.
Breasts	Nurture, love, mother love, giving and receiving nurturing, abuse trauma, relationship with close family members.
Bunions	Feeling vulnerable and exposed in your quest to move away from family values. Stubbornness, "I will show you." Pushing too hard—can only have fun when working hard.
Cheeks	Insecurities. Feel intimidated by authority and confrontation.
Chest	Feel pushed away by a mother and pushing people away. Negative association with love.

Chin	Worthiness, anger related to words you cannot express. Feel betrayed yet unable to say anything about it. Your truth is not believed.
Ear	What don't you want to hear, need to block out; who or what? Fear of confrontation. Feel disempowered by influential people.
Elbow	Poor personal boundaries. Need to push people away. Hardening of the attitude. Indecisiveness, "Should I, or shouldn't I?" Lack of passion related to what you do in life. Elbow problems are related to feeling very indecisive. Not knowing whether to leave or continue a project, job, or relationship. Feeling obligated to see things through however, even though there is no benefit for you.
Eyebrows	Need to be different than others. Don't feel unique and good enough as you are. Lack of acknowledgement and praise.
Eyes	Seeing truth, resistance to not seeing your environment, too much responsibility, wanting to hide. Related to birth trauma.
Fat	Protection. Being unattractive = feeling safe. Trauma related to scarcity such as food, love, and protection. Trauma related to someone threatening you in the past. Love and relationships = toxicity.
Feet	Stepping forward, control, direction, stubbornness, feel controlled and out of control, resistance to change, fear of moving away from family and family values.

Fingers	Feel unsure where you fit in, needing to establish your identity, to be validated, do not feel supported when doing things. Holding back secrets, direction in life, passion. See the Fingers section.
Forehead	Feel conflicted and angry due to current circumstances and people in your immediate environment. Feel like losing control.
Fungus	Resentment related to a mother / feminine figure. Abandonment trauma.
Glands	Feeling unable to express boundaries. Holding back anger as a result of recent circumstances. Represents how you feel about your situation.
Gums	Feeling attacked, unsupported when making decisions. Feel unable to change / break away from unhealthy circumstances. Anger is your best defense.
Hair	How you feel about yourself. Feeling unprotected. Need to get away / escape circumstances or someone. Feel controlled and threatened. Disassociated from feelings.
Hands	Blocks around receiving, giving, delegating without guilt, understanding how you feel when you are working (such as in the workplace).
Heart	Giving and receiving of love and nurturing. The Left side ventricle is related to receiving. The right-side ventricle is related to giving. Also related to one's territory and competitiveness.
Hip	Balance and moving forward, being flexible, relationship problems, sexuality, confidence in personal relationships.

Infection	Resentment and anger grown out of control. Disgusted with self, feeling shame and suppressing feelings of panic.
Intestines	Store old abuse, store resentment, anger, vengeance, injustice, and betrayal within close relationships.
Jaw	How one expresses oneself to parents—what is the conflict?
Kidney	Resentment, anger, not letting go, toxic relationships.
Knees	Moving forward, making big changes, fear of what others might think if you follow your own beliefs and values. Fear of stepping into influential roles. Feel pushed down and controlled by a feminine figure.
Cut on Knee	Your goals and needs are attacked, criticized and unsupported by influential people.
Lips	Feeling insecure and overly aware of how others view you. Fear and tension related to what you need to say. You don't trust your own judgment.
Liver	Regret, resentment, guilt because of what one cannot change. Anger related to feeling suppressed, loss of identity.
Lungs	Grief, depression, sorrow, lack of joy, feeling smothered, suppressed and controlled by those you rely on for love.
Lymph nodes	Unable to let go of toxic relationships, love is toxic and unhealthy, but I can't let it go. Unable to forgive. Anger is my power and strength.
Muscles	Knowing what is good / bad for oneself. Self-sabotaging health

	and happiness. Stuck in unhealthy / undesirable circumstances and feeling helpless to change it. Feeling under attack. How one feels about oneself, stubbornness, having to be right, holding on to guilt.
Myelin Sheath	Trauma related to communication. Blocking what you see and sense in your environment. Self-sabotage of personal progress. Love in your life feels toxic, stressful, and invasive.
Nails	Feeling unprotected, controlled, and manipulated by authority.
Neck	Rigidity, not able to make decisions, resisting your environment. Feel vulnerable and out of your depth within circumstances and relationships. Not allowed to be with someone else.
Nerves	Communication trauma. Ability to communicate is being controlled and manipulated by authority.
Nose	(See Sinus) Personal power, how strong do you feel when outside of your comfort zone? Trauma related to intuition and psychic abilities. Your character feels under attack.
Ovaries	Relationship with femininity. Being too masculine in your approach to live. It is not safe to feel feminine. Unresolved stress with a mother figure.
Parasites	Boundary issues, invasion, not feeling worthy of saying "no."
Pelvis	Ancestral trauma related to sexual abuse, feeling unimportant, cannot stand your ground, feel powerless.

Rashes	Built-up trauma related to fear of confrontation, verbal or physical abuse. Take things too personally.
Ribs	Feel ignored by family, unable to protect what matters to me.
Shoulders	Carrying responsibility (Financial / Family) / guilt about having fun.
Sinus / Blocked	Trauma related to intuition and psychic abilities. Feel offended and invaded by environment. Feel rejected and abandoned. Disconnected from feeling joy.
Skin	Irritation, sensitivity to specific issues / people, lack of protection, poor personal boundaries, holding on to anger and resentment, feeling vulnerable.
Spine	Structure, direction in life, burdens, financial responsibility, sexuality, reproducing, breadwinner.
Stomach	Unresolved stress with mother. Controlling, smothering fear-based love.
Swelling	Boundary failures resulted in anger and feeling helpless. You are not expressing clear boundaries.
Teeth	How supported and protected you felt during your childhood and womb stages.
Tendon	There is urgency to what you want to do, feel pressured. Everyone is watching my every move.
Testicles	Relationship with father is strained. Feeling suppressed by a dominant female figure. Unresolved stress with a child or the child that never came.
Tongue	You are not sharing your opinion. Feel silenced by authority.

Veins	Feels blocked around receiving love and support. Receiving may have equaled feeling obligated, controlled. Love = abuse / lack.
Virus	Worthiness, disappointment, self-punishment, poor personal boundaries, having to fight for respect and understanding.
Warts	Feeling resentful toward influential people for projecting too much responsibility onto you. People in your life feel energetically parasitic. Feelings of resentment have grown out of control.
Wrists	Feel that you are the buffer between two people, feeling caught in the middle of something. Fear of failure.

About the Author

Evette Rose is an Author, Life Coach, Founder of Unfuck Your Life, Metaphysical Anatomy Technique (M.A.T) development company and founder of several books. Evette was born in South Africa and grew up in Namibia, West Africa. She then moved to Australia, lived in Vanuatu and Bali. She is best known for her work in helping people to resolve trauma from their past and freeing them to live successful and fulfilling lives. Evette's work is

drawn from her own personal experience of moving from a difficult past into a well-balanced life and career. Evette's philosophy is that we, as a human race, are not destined to live our lives in pain because of past trauma or abuse. We often suppress our ability to complete or heal trauma naturally. In today's society, we often suppress our pain in order to keep up with life and avoid being left behind. Fortunately, through gentle therapy, this natural internal healing instinct can be restored. Writing her books has helped Evette reach out to other people who need love, support, and someone to relate to. She shares her experiences with the world, hoping it will help people heal and provide encouragement and reassurance when they need it most. Evette now travels the world teaching personal development seminars and continues her research journey. She has been to well over 40 countries and worked with thousands of people.

References

https://psychlabs.ryerson.ca/caplab/is-difficulty-concentrating-making-your-worry-and-anxiety-worse-by-leah-sack/#:~:text=Generalized%20anxiety%20disorder%20(GAD)%20is,become%20distracted%20by%20their%20worry.

https://www.healthline.com/health/anxiety/social-phobia#treatment

https://www.nhs.uk/mental-health/conditions/social-anxiety/#:~:text=Social%20anxiety%20is%20more%20than,before%2C%20during%20and%20after%20them.

https://www.nhs.uk/mental-health/conditions/social-anxiety/#:~:text=Social%20anxiety%20is%20more%20than,before%2C%20during%20and%20after%20them.

https://www.nimh.nih.gov/health/publications/generalized-anxiety-disordergad#:~:text=What%20is%20generalized%20anxiety%20disorder,reason%20to%20worry%20about%20them.

https://www.talkspace.com/blog/psychosomatic-disorders-definition-symptoms/

https://integrativepsych.co/new-blog/anxiety-specialist-five-towns

https://my.clevelandclinic.org/health/diseases/21521-psychosomatic-disorder

https://pubmed.ncbi.nlm.nih.gov/28866901/#:~:text=Psychosomatic%20disorder%20is%20a%20condition,system%20and%20the%20biochemical%20response.

https://www.healthline.com/health/anxiety/anxiety-triggers

https://medium.com/invisible-illness/anxiety-through-the-ages-616b96044dbc

https://www.psychotherapynetworker.org/magazine/article/92/a-brief-history-of-anxiety

https://www.healthline.com/health/grounding-techniques

https://www.calmclinic.com/brief-history-of-anxiety

https://www.medicalnewstoday.com/articles/grounding-techniques#summary

https://www.therapistaid.com/tools/anxiety/none

https://www.therapistaid.com/therapy-articles/anxiety/none

https://www.apa.org/topics/stress/body#:~:text=Excess%20amounts%20of%20cortisol%20can,of%20the%20male%20reproductive%20system.&text=Chronic%20stress%2C%20ongoing%20stress%20over,cause%20erectile%20dysfunction%20or%20impotence.

https://www.sunshineclinic.org/blog/how-stress-affects-your-immune-system/#:~:text=Many%20factors%20contribute%20to%20stress,normal%20white%20blood%20cell%20communication.

https://www.health.harvard.edu/mind-and-mood/recognizing-and-easing-the-physical-symptoms-of-anxiety

https://www.medicalnewstoday.com/articles/326646

https://www.rosehillcenter.org/mental-health-blog/10-reasons-you-may-have-the-inability-to-relax/

https://adaa.org/learn-from-us/from-the-experts/blog-posts/consumer/thoughts-are-just-thoughts

https://www.bbc.com/future/article/20160928-how-anxiety-warps-your-perception

https://my.clevelandclinic.org/health/diseases/21543-sleep-anxiety#:~:text=Sleep%20anxiety%20is%20a%20feeling%20of%20fear%20or%20stress%20about,sleep%20problems%20are%20both%20treatable.

https://www.sicknotweak.com/2017/08/mental-illness-not-character-flaw/

https://www.health.harvard.edu/blog/do-i-have-anxiety-or-worry-whats-the-difference-2018072314303

https://khealth.com/learn/fatigue/can-anxiety-cause-fatigue/#:~:text=Anxiety%20can%20lead%20to%20muscle,to%20feelings%2020of%20physical%20fatigue.

https://researchportal.helsinki.fi/en/publications/brain-plasticity-modulator-p75-neurotrophin-receptor-and-its-mech

https://www.ncbi.nlm.nih.gov/pmc/articles/PMC7352860/

- Albert-Gascó H, Ros-Bernal F, Castillo-Gómez E, Olucha-Bordonau FE. MAP/ERK Signaling in Developing Cognitive and Emotional Function and Its Effect on Pathological and Neurodegenerative Processes. Int J Mol Sci. 2020 Jun 23;21(12):4471. doi: 10.3390/ijms21124471. PMID: 32586047; PMCID: PMC7352860.

https://pubmed.ncbi.nlm.nih.gov/22869608/
- Alexander N, Rosenlöcher F, Stalder T, Linke J, Distler W, Morgner J, Kirschbaum C. Impact of antenatal synthetic glucocorticoid exposure on endocrine stress reactivity in term-born children. J Clin Endocrinol Metab. 2012 Oct;97(10):3538-44. doi: 10.1210/jc.2012-1970. Epub 2012 Aug 6. PMID: 22869608.

- Koyanagi, T., Horimoto, N., Maeda, H., Kukita, J., Minami, T., Ueda, K., & Nakano, H. (2016). Abnormal Behavioral Patterns in the Human Fetus at Term: Correlation with Lesion Sites in the Central Nervous System after Birth. Journal of Child Neurology. https://doi.org/10.1177/088307389300800103

- Thau L, Gandhi J, Sharma S. Physiology, Cortisol. [Updated 2022 Aug 29]. In: StatPearls [Internet]. Treasure Island (FL): StatPearls Publishing; 2022 Jan-. Available from: https://www.ncbi.nlm.nih.gov/books/NBK538239/

Made in the USA
Columbia, SC
19 June 2023

17980716R00117